Successful
Ambitions
Cooper R. Wade

COOPER WADE
ENTERPRISES

Published in the United States of America
Seattle, Washington, 2016
CreateSpace Publishing
		An Amazon Company

ISBN: 1522949461
ISBN 13: 9781522949466
Library of Congress Control Number: **XXXXX (Pending)**
LCCN Imprint Name: **City and State (Pending)**

This book is dedicated to those who have the dedication, motivation, and confidence to achieve their dreams.

This book is also dedicated to my family and close friends who have helped me achieve my dreams.

Acknowledgments

I would like to take the opportunity to thank everyone who has played a part in many of my ideas, projects, and companies along this journey.

I would like to especially thank everyone in my family for the encouragement to chase after my dreams.

I would also like to thank Mike Coulson and his family for the guidance and leadership they have shown me.

Successful Ambitions—Cooper R. Wade

Some Words from Me to You

I assume that if you're reading this book you yearn to be successful one day. I assume that you're self-motivated—you've shown me this because you're reading these words right now. I assume that you have a vision of where you want to be one day.

I can't tell you exactly what to do in order to accomplish this. Your path is completely different from mine. I can tell you how I went about my personal accomplishments, but yours are something only you can determine.

I'm far from ever stopping in my desire to achieve success and learn from my mistakes. That will only happen when I stop breathing. You have to want to be successful as badly as you want to breathe. Once you can find that, you'll do well.

I believe the insights you'll discover while reading this book are all determined by yourself. You have only one life to live, so you might as well change the world for the better if you have the chance. Do something people will remember you for. Make a difference. Make an impact on someone's life. These were the things I grew up hearing. My parents always told me to dream and then go for it. If someone else could do it, what was keeping me from doing it? I want to impart this view of life to you. I want to help instill that intrinsic motivation into you so that you can one day be the difference maker that the world is looking for.

You can be whatever religion you choose. I choose to believe in the one true God. Before I lose some of you, please hear me out. I am a true and firm Southern Baptist young man. I love Jesus Christ. I believe that God has a plan and a purpose for my life. I also believe that He has a plan and a purpose for you as well.

I have had lots of things happen in my twenty years on planet Earth. I have been through freedom and life-threatening situations. A lot of them. These situations are a story for another time. My point is that I've been through a lot of these experiences, but I've also made it through all of them. I have also learned a lot from each one. But every time something happens, I realize the same thing. God has a plan and a purpose for me. I may fail at a lot of the different things I pursue, but He has a plan for me. There are some instances that have happened where I know there is something He has in store. I don't know what it is. I can tell you there is a plan. I can also tell you that He has a plan for you. This is where I find my motivation to keep going. Every time things get hard, I know it is making me stronger. I know one day I will be better for it. I don't always learn a lesson right away, but it will come in time.

For all my ambitious and determined people out there, I pray that you will follow this same moral. I know there is something He has in store. I want you to know that too. You wouldn't be here reading this if He didn't.

Hopefully you can see my main topic is motivation. That's the fuel for your fire. That's what will keep you driving for success.

I assume that a large amount of my readers are young adults—college students and teenagers. I know how it feels to come through high school and see the world as your playground. You have lots of ambitious plans on your horizon. This can come to an abrupt halt as soon as you emerge into the "real world," as they call it. You may have college debt, car payments, and other expenses. Don't let your current situation bring you down simply because you aren't used to it. Keep your head up, and remember to not become satisfied with your current situation. Strive to do more, achieve more, and learn more.

I want this book to help fuel your drive for success. I want to see some of my readers become the next world changers. I want you to see my humble beginnings and think to yourself that you can do it too. There will be those who will say you can't, but I would beg to differ. People who say you can't are the people that won't themselves.

God bless.

Contents

1
Introduction: Purpose

Everything is intentional. Ask me why I do something, and I'll have an answer. After you read this book, I hope you'll have the inspiration and guidance to figure out where you're going.

There is a purpose to everything.

There is a purpose for me.

There is a purpose for you.

There is a purpose for everything that happens along our individual, ambitious paths.

Whether or not you believe me, there is in fact a purpose for this very book.

Hello, I'm Cooper Wade. I am currently a twenty-year-old southern boy. I grew up with dreams and aspirations just as most kids do. The only difference is I still dream. I dream every day about new ideas, about places I want to go, about what my future family will be like. Dreaming is a healthy part of growing and developing. It allows us to ponder on the future and what it holds for each of us.

I would like you to know that there are two types of people in this world. There are dreamers and visionaries. Dreamers can come up with some pretty amazing things, but it takes a dedicated person to take a dream and turn it into a vision. A vision is something you foresee. It is your path of what you want created.

I would like to add here that I'm a futurist. I believe that change is always a positive experience more often than not. The only problem is that everyone perceives change differently. Everyone sees everything differently. You can thank your paradigm for that one. This is how each one of us accepts and defines information. I may know something would work where you may think not. These are our paradigms in action. So as you read, please pay attention to this topic, because hopefully by the end you see the importance of accepting change.

I would call myself a dreamer, but also a visionary. I've always wanted to become successful in many different ways. I had all kinds of interests growing up. I wanted to do it all. So far I have gotten the chance to try my hand at most of it. One lesson that helped me the most was when a mentor of mine wouldn't make a decision for me. He was my college physics professor, and he couldn't tell me what I was supposed to do after college.

He said, "The purpose of you being in college is so you can learn something. Something that helps you go to work and never work a day in your life."

At that moment, during my sophomore year of college, I knew I was on the right track. I personally loved everything about physics. It was the one subject where I was able to create and ask why. The one field of study where I could find the solution to why. I loved (and still love) having the ability to create.

This man knew what he was saying. Find something you like; explore it. Do you find satisfaction in doing this? Do you enjoy it? I believe if you can't enjoy your work, then maybe you need to sit back and reconsider some things.

Keep in mind, your purpose may not lie within this path in your life. I have found that my path lies somewhere along innovation and entrepreneurship. I don't go to work every day and plug in physics equations and test the theory of atmospheric penetration of rockets using the moon's gravity to propel them toward Mars. Granted, I could do it if necessary, but I think you get the point. I gained countless problem-solving skills through this educational focus. I have used them every day at every job I have ever worked. I am a physicist by trade and an entrepreneur by heart. It has made me a great leader because of my decision-making skills.

I assume there is a decent audience of young adults probably still in school who are reading this as well as older, more experienced adults. To the younger ones, your educational focus does not define you. The Fortune 500 companies I have worked for (or with) hire based on *you*. They care about what's inside you. An engineer with an aeronautical engineering master's degree brings something different to being a manager than someone with a business degree. There is no right or wrong way to go. You don't have to have fancy degrees from prestigious schools. It may help, but companies tend to be very relational businesses. By relational, I mean that they want to know you. Once they know what you're capable of, they will promote from within. You're not as much of a risk because they know what you bring to the table. You can work your way up rather easily with proper dedication and commitment.

Speaking of purpose, like I said, this book has a couple. You'll get to read about my story, from growing up and getting into business at a young age to where I currently sit here in Orlando, Florida. My ambition has taken me everywhere from Washington, DC to Los Angeles, and even to Costa Rica. If I put my mind to something, you better bet I'm going to make it happen. Then we will define success and failure not as the world sees them, but how doers and ambitious individuals should see them. We will then move into where you take your ideas—what happens next. There is a general process to how you will go about these new endeavors; some are fast and some are slow. Again, there is no wrong way. The book then finishes from the perspective of a person who is achieving success, but still trying to get the new business off the ground. I'll tell you about emerging business leadership and propelling your company's growth to remain on the cutting edge.

The main reason I wrote this book was to change up the genre I am writing for. Typically books about success are written from the point of view of an adult who has successfully innovated in some way, and he or she is reflecting back on the journey. I wanted to change that. My goal is to write for mainly young adults who see the world like I do, as an opportunity. I want to give you a personal feel into what it is like to be ambitious at fourteen years old and to be successful by twenty. I wanted to better relate to people like myself. I understand how negativity can feel as well as your first sale. I know how hard it can be to read books about these millionaires who built massive companies seemingly overnight. Thankfully I know a handful of them, and I can share with you some of their insights as well. I want you to see what it's like to experience all this as it happens.

I want this to be an inspiring experience for you. I want you to be energized after reading this and to feel empowered to set forth and make your dreams a reality. I want this to provide you with a type of guide, where you can take ideas or suggestions and think about them.

2
This Is Me:
Take It or Leave It

Please stand clear of the doors. *¡Por favor manténgase alejado de las puertas!*

OK, now that we have our disclaimers out of the way, I can actually get started. You guys hold on because this ride will have its ups and downs. So sit back and relax as we climb to an altitude of twenty thousand feet on our way to success, and we will get there when we get there.

Right now I sit here at twenty years old. I sit here in the middle of Florida. There are palm trees all around, sand between my toes, and the soft noise of water rolling up on the shore. Every now and then I look up to see a glowing castle filled with inspiration across the lagoon. The boats travel to and fro, taking people on their merry way. Occasionally, the sky becomes lit with large flashes of light that awe everyone within reach, and families and children get wide-eyed taking a picture with a mouse in suspenders. If you haven't realized at this point from the world-famous monorail disclaimer, well…I work at Disney World.

I know what you're thinking: "That doesn't sound so bad." Right? It's not that it's bad, but if you're like me, then you want to have some sort of a plan to ensure you're on the right path. The one thing that has become reality is that for those of us who are ambitious, there is no foreseeable future.

So again, I sit here contemplating what is to come. The one thing no one knows except the man above. No sense worrying about it if it's meant to be His will. It's not as easy as paying someone five dollars to look at your hand and make up a generalized opinion. The future can be a scary thing for anyone. From where I'm at, things look pretty bright and inspiring. Now, granted, I am watching some neat fireworks across the Seven Seas Lagoon where there's a castle lit up in Christmas-like fashion as Tinker Bell flies over the onlookers. You can't get a whole lot more inspiring than that right there.

But to get this show on the road, as we may say, allow me to introduce myself. I feel like you should know some of my past before I get to the good parts. Although it is important to remember your past, realize that your past never defines your future. You can be as average, normal, boring, weird, strange, or whatever word people can create for you. But this will never affect your future. Your future is only affected by you. Certainly, people can come along and try to ruin things for you and something bad may happen where your life seems to end for about ten seconds. I've had these moments where I needed a friend to come along and slap me until I realize the world isn't over and I still have a job to do.

My name is Cooper Wade. I was born in Little Rock, Arkansas to a lovely couple by the names of Guy and Cara, with whom I am now stuck for the rest of my life. I love my family dearly, as you will see through some of my stories, especially the ones depicting how well my brothers and I got along at a young age. Boys will be boys, right? But really, I was blessed to have two younger brothers who, whether they knew it or not, were influencing me toward becoming a leader. I also had a great set of grandparents who encouraged me in every way they could. I would have to say that my grandpa was my greatest life mentor. He influenced every inch of my direction in life. Overall, my family situation was pretty nice. I'm very grateful for this.

As a child I was a little runt at times. I caused trouble, as all little boys did. I grew up on a street that had eleven kids living in eleven houses. Our family had the house at the top of our cove on the hill. It seemed as though every day we would all meet up in the cove as we came up with what to do that day. The usual was either messing with the girls that lived down the street or playing some form of hide-and-seek. We also developed our own small city where we made coins from tree branches and placed our label on them. There it was—a great idea was born! This was the start of a new era. I was to become president; my destiny was now instilled in my mind. I knew what I had to do.

Wait a minute. No, no—that's not how the rest of my life fell into place. I went on, possibly the next day, back to being that usual child. The neighbors and I were playing basketball on our driveway one day when we looked down the hill to see smoke rising from the backyard of one of those girls' houses. Let me remind you, at eight years old, girls still had cooties. But as all young boys would, we ran down to see the fire. And there it sat, a bright force to be reckoned with. The older and more mature young men, including myself, walked back up the hill. My younger brother Carter decided to stay a little longer. He came running up behind us after he had "helped" the fire. By that, we came to understand, he meant he had set the neighbor's backyard on fire in the middle of October. Our initial reaction was to go to the nearest house, where our neighbor seemed to live in his garage as he fixed his cars every other day. He wasn't buying the story. Long story short, that yard grew back as green as could be. It also somehow gained two dogs and a fence in the meantime. But to finish it all out, three houses got sold that year out of eleven (including the ones on either side of that yard). That's when we realized our true calling to become entrepreneurs. We weren't even nine yet, and we'd sold three houses. It was clear we were destined for greatness.

　　We continued to do business at our family yard sale, where my youngest brother had the great idea to sell cold drinks to people who came to shop our assortment of unique oddities. This is where our creative marketing plan shocked the world. We learned how to draw customers in quick and then show them the strings attached. The sign on the mailbox read, "Free Cokes for a Dollar." Yes, ladies and gentlemen, you read that correctly. You have to admit, it got your attention. Then people would see my six-year-old brother innocently sitting there and couldn't just walk past. That day we made a killing of around twenty-four dollars, which was rollin' pretty good for a couple of kids. We had to decline all the television offers, though, because we were concerned about our possible viral popularity.

Nonetheless, we were on the way to stardom. Then this period called middle school set in, and it was time for a real job. I was officially on the job market, searching high and low, but I quickly found I was overqualified for most positions so I went back into self-employment. I started mowing lawns and cleaning houses. The neighbors and I also built a two-story fort in the backyard that functioned as our metal recycling center. We went around the neighborhood and the entire town for that matter, collecting cans in the back of my grandfather's pickup. We would then bring them all to my backyard to smash them up and haul them off. Business seemed to be booming. We had a nice collection of fire extinguishers and even a whole car's exhaust. This stuff was so neat to a middle schooler we almost didn't want to throw it away. It took a couple days, but we were finally discovered to not have the proper licenses in order to be operating a neighborhood-wide recycling center out of a tree house in the backyard of a middle-upper-class neighborhood. We had neglected to provide the needed documents for my parents to accept the new business plan. A couple truckloads and a trailer took care of our backyard. As for the tree house, well, it was returned to being just a tree house. And just like that, I went from being a CEO back to reality and the classified sections.

I honestly enjoy moments like these, because they allow you to sit back and analyze where you're going and where you want to be.

The next step in my life was a rather large one. As with everything great, I started small. I wanted something that I could make a little larger return on. The idea was born on a small lake in Hot Springs, Arkansas. I remember it like it was yesterday. I was sitting out by the lake with my family and a good friend, and I started playing with a metal bottle cap in my hands. This is when I started thinking about the bottle cap as a piece of art rather than its intended use. I wanted this to be more than something that got tossed in a trash can. In fact, I decided I would like to wear this on my neck. So, I knew where I needed to start.

I decided to make bottle cap necklaces out of string and chain to sell. This was when the idea developed into something more. About a week later, I introduced earrings featuring retro bottle caps from older brands as well as modern companies. At a surprising rate, these earrings became increasingly popular, all by word of mouth. This was when I needed a way to market to more people. What better way than social media and the Internet?

Business started developing when I decided to spend the money to get a lawyer and an accountant, and within a week I had my business license. We purchased some web space and went to work on copyrighting slogans, names, designs, and so on. The next step was to create a logo: challenge accepted.

Within two weeks' time, I had developed a small, successful online business for around $450. A small price to pay for endless possibilities. Shortly after designing the logo, I got attention from people seeing the design at school. It was then that I started getting requests from people to place it on a T-shirt in a similar fashion to the large clothing designer Polo.

Business grew quickly. I started getting letters and phone calls from companies like Google, Facebook, and Twitter. My common sense told me I needed to take action if I wanted the business to succeed. I started a marketing and advertising campaign that targeted specific age ranges and regions of possible customers. It was amazing to be able to harness technology that could specify possible customers all the way down to the individual. Before we knew it, Facebook was running ads in multiple states, and Google had us on the top of the search query. Within the next three months, we began shipping across the nation to places such as Maryland and Alabama.

The growth was an amazing experience! We had the best problem to have, which was trying to produce enough to keep up with the orders. I switched producers three times and got to turn the tables to where companies were bidding for our business.

All successful business owners have had that moment where they know their work has paid off. For me it wasn't so much the financial aspect as it was seeing the business grow. I realized it when one day the local news stations were calling to get times to film interviews. At fifteen this is an exciting thing but also very scary. I also went on the next year as a freshman to speak to students at my high school about new businesses and how I got started. I enjoyed getting to show others how they could make their dreams a reality.

It was a great experience that lasted about four years. We kept expanding as high school ended and college began. Business was all right. We even merged to take over another small clothing line. We had a custom trailer made for tailgating outfitted with a television, a sound system, clothing stock, and a checkout area. But, fortunately, I wanted to focus on college classes so I decided to sell everything from the clothing company. We closed up shop, and I waited for the next idea.

Thankfully, starting shortly after the first year of this four-year journey in the clothing business, I had branched out into a different industry and started working on my first invention. Alternative energy had begun to pique my interest. Growing up I had always heard talk on television about America's growing energy problem. It made me start thinking about how this would be a big issue when I became an adult. So, I started researching many different forms of energy creation. I read lots of books on the subject, which was ironic because I hated reading with a passion. But when it came to reading something that I actually wanted to learn, I loved it. I learned many things about many different researchers, but one stood out among the rest. Leonardo da Vinci was a favorite of mine. His focuses on perpetual motion and efficiency were interesting subjects.

All this research sparked thinking. I started thinking about how to make electrical devices more efficient. I ended up, after many months of concepts and diagrams, with a concept of an electric car centered on a key operating system. I began presenting this idea to numerous potential investors and friends. The project received lots of attention, but never got off the ground other than small prototype designs. The physics behind the idea assumed too many factors that made some people weary. I didn't let that stop me.

As I entered college, like I said, I wanted to sell off my company's assets so I could focus on school. So I slowly did, as I started a new job as the university's head team manager for the football department. This job was pretty exciting. I got to meet many awesome people and experience many new things along the way. I mostly stuck with this job to be able to stay around the sport. I wasn't quite ready to leave yet. As I went on trips for the away games, I continued to research new ideas.

Over the first few months of college I came up with multiple ideas, which my physics and business professors worked with me on. But I had one problem. I didn't have enough funding for my expensive projects. So I decided to go about it a different way.

I realized I had found my problem: how to get the money. You're probably thinking to yourself, "Well duh, doesn't everyone have that problem?" You aren't wrong. I kept thinking of ways to start a small temporary business to sell a very basic product for a short amount of time. I thought this would raise the capital I needed for my projects. Instead, I started a private investment holdings company, which invested in similar business plans that fell along our company's interests. Since I wanted to develop technology related to energy, those were the types of new businesses we were interested in.

Aurelia Enterprises Inc. was our young company. We started with two ideas. One was from a group of aerospace engineers. They had developed a drone that could fly for up to four years at around 80,000–100,000 feet. This drone could set up a secure wireless communications network for militaries to use in case of an infrastructure meltdown. Now you're probably wondering why we invested in a military technology group. They were a very innovative group of guys who also used new forms of electricity storage for the drone. When an idea comes along with lots of potential, you're not going to turn it down.

The second company was a small group in China. They owned some small shipyard docks on the Yangtze River. They were looking for some modest capital to develop a large energy-efficient farming community in rural China. After just two years, they now have their eyes set on being the largest farm of its kind in the world, standing at over 100,000 acres.

These ideas were within our current price range. They allowed us to grow to where we could fund our own ideas and research. I continued to research perpetual motion and energy efficiency while in college. As the company progressed, I decided to make a major change. We changed our name to Cooper Wade Enterprises and started to plan funding for our first business.

After about three months, we opened our first wholly owned subsidiary, Solaire Energy Group. My best friend, who was an energy-efficiency engineer for the city, and I opened up shop. We started with a large flatbed truck, an office, and a warehouse. We quickly went to work however we could manage. Our original business model was to install and service solar panels and wind turbines. The business gained lots of attention during our first few months from state representatives and large companies. We began negotiating contracts worth up to eight million dollars. These were numbers we weren't used to seeing, especially during the first two months of business. We eventually broadened our services to designing custom applications. We began with a five-story wind and solar tower that quickly became the talk of the town. So needless to say, our marketing was doing itself. Currently we are trying to restructure Solaire Energy Group to broaden our engineering services even more.

This is where you're probably wondering what I'm doing at Disney World, right? Well, I came here to see what it's like working for a large, successful company. I wanted to learn how they conducted business and what made them successful. I work in merchandise as a trainer for new cast members. I wanted to be different and do what I love, which is designing and engineering new things.

Long story short, I became a Disney Inventor when I designed an attraction based on one of my inventions. The idea got passed along to the intellectual properties division. It gained lots of attention along the way. Later, I found out that it had made its way into Imagineering. To spring forward in time a bit, the idea is now protected as Disney's intellectual property. There is a possibility that the attraction may be built. That's all I wanted.

So now I am trying my best here at Disney to see where my path takes me. I still own my businesses based in Arkansas. Thankfully, I have some trusted friends and family to help run it. My life has been quite a journey to getting to where I'm at, but the key to it all has been motivation and self-determination. Each and every time, I believed in what I was doing. Sometimes you'll be the only believer in yourself.

3
The Visual Story

I thought it would be nice if I included some pictures for you from my past endeavors. After all, picture books are my favorite. I hope this helps you to see a little better how I went about developing my ideas.

One thing I do want you to try and recognize is the changes in each idea and how they became more defined along the way. I assure you that the rest of this book expands on these changes, but realize where each idea came from and see how they evolved depending on different needs. Enjoy.

Well, here it is—the very first logo and slogan that I came up with for my first business. At fourteen years old, I figured all people named their businesses after themselves. My nickname was Coop, so I figured this was an acceptable fit. Also, I couldn't think of anything better than the sunset on the beach. And this awesome logo was born. This was used for the clothing company I told you about.

My goal was to have a laid-back and relaxed company. I wanted to evoke a certain feeling when people saw my logo for the first time. I quickly created the term "the relaxer," which was who our clothes and jewelry were marketed toward.

Your goal for your logo is to create a quick reference of what your company is. You want to find a symbol that represents what you're about. A palm tree and sunset accomplished just that.

Below you can see some of our products as we began to move into the clothing business. This was our simple and humble beginning.

We started with what was easy and most affordable on our budget. Hats and T-shirts were the answer. As they gained popularity, I decided to move into more colors. We offered up to thirty-two different colors, twelve of which were available in eco-friendly materials such as bamboo. Our next step was to broaden our horizons with different products, so we began to offer polo-style business casual shirts.

Then it was time to become something different. We had already unleashed men's swimming trunks and ladies' jackets by now. What was something that many people had never seen before? That's it! I went back to the bamboo idea. It was perfect for a beach-themed company. I thought, let's make polo-style shirts out of bamboo. So, we did.

We brought out a series that came in three colors. These shirts were made of a different type of thread. It was actually made of bamboo charcoal woven with cotton fibers. At the time, this was one of the most advanced ways of producing material, but also one of the most expensive. We still released the product, and yes, there was a trade-off. Bamboo is one of the softest materials I have ever felt, but it came at a price for our customers at around $59.95. It was also one of the most environmentally friendly and efficient pieces of clothing on the market, and it even had an SPF rating of 20!

Now a main focus of a business is the perception of your company to its customers, correct? Our main business was conducted online or in person, as most businesses operate. I chose to focus more attention on our website, mainly because it is more affordable than operating a retail clothing outlet. Our website became the face of our business.

Our website was called coopscasual.com. We directed our customers there so they could see our product offerings if they were not physically available. The website featured a page about how we got started as a brand, our online store, and a social networking page that was added later. Having our sales primarily online allowed us to configure shipping labels and send packages very easily. So not only did it allow us to be more accessible, but to also run the business from one location. You're probably wondering how we had an individual social network. This was an experimental option that I was playing

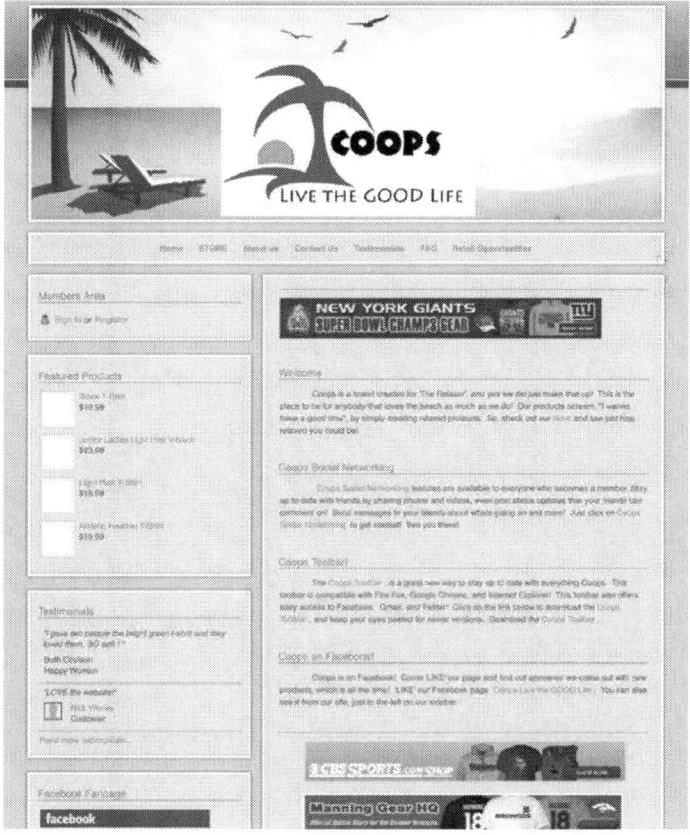

with to see how effective having members would be. To my surprise it worked very well and was a good place where we could offer member discounts on items as an incentive. Sometimes members met their friends on our website and started conversations about our products. It was a very helpful tool.

One of my proudest moments was when we received our first website advertisements. Displayed on our page were the New York Giants at the top, and CBS Sports and the Denver Broncos at the bottom. What was even more awesome was when the New York Giants won the Super Bowl later that season. We got to place a special advertisement saying, "Official Online Store of the New York Giants." This was the high point of the clothing business before I let it go a few years later.

My next business, Aurelia Enterprises Inc., followed about a year later. I wanted to move into a field in which I had an interest in pursuing a career. I want to be somewhere on the cutting edge. I want to be at the forefront of innovation.

I have always loved pursuing my own ideas and projects, but as I got older, my projects seemed to get more expensive. It's easy for that to happen when you're dealing with technology. This company was my solution. I wanted to fund other people's ideas at a fraction of the cost in order to earn a profit. Then, in return, I'd reinvest into other business plans or our own. This was my solution for raising capital for my own projects.

It made sense to run this business exclusively online. If the sole purpose was to gain capital, why would I spend money for an office when I didn't need one? I learned how to build a website on my own and wrote all the website copy myself. I probably spent about twenty hours per week on just website design, but I ended up with what I wanted. The goal was to send a clear message about our purpose as a company. We didn't sell a product; we didn't sell a service. We wanted to be an informational source. The website functioned as the face of our business. Once again, this is one of the most affordable tools an entrepreneur or small business owner can utilize.

Believe it or not, I actually designed this whole website on a charter bus on the way to an away college football game in Oklahoma. I'm very proud of this design. I felt like it gave our company a very professional appeal.

Having a website also allowed us to connect to our clients better. On the site we included our four main goals and focuses, which were world markets, innovation, building industry, and effective risk taking. We also had another page that described how the company got started and where our name came from. The name *Aurelia* came from an old Spanish treasure fleet ship that has never been recovered. It's said it would be the most valuable ship if found. This led to the only problem I ended up having: no one knew how to spell *Aurelia*. Originally, I loved the story behind the name, but I eventually came to the realization that it needed to change. Along with this change, I wanted to make an even bigger change. I figured if I was going to change the name, I would also change the way the company was perceived. I wanted to create a new, bolder look for the business. If I was going to put my name on it, I wanted it to be on the cutting edge.

As the new website was unfolding, I decided to change up the way our company was perceived. I decided to film our first informative video to tell everyone what we're all about. You can still view it online at cooperwadeenterprises.com. In the video you'll see our international spokesperson, national spokesperson, and myself. You'll also get to hear about the different businesses we're involved in.

Here you can see the design of the new website when we first released it. We came out with many new features, like the video I mentioned. We also had a company news section and stock-price graph on the top right side of the home page. This greatly affected our company's impact by providing us with more credibility.

It was about a half year later that I started my new business venture, Solaire Energy Group. I choreographed these changes so that as we began the new company path, we could also show how we were achieving it. We added the web page for Solaire to our main site.

We started by providing ourselves with the necessary tools we needed to get the job done. I figured our first line of business was to get a utility truck and begin marketing our company.

Well, here's me smiling ear to ear sitting on the flatbed. I can't tell you how exciting it is seeing your dream coming together. It's a feeling that never gets old. Luckily, it wasn't hard for me to expand, due to a family-owned farm. We had plenty of space to store tools and equipment. We ended up with a large two-story warehouse and workshop combination. A few months later we added our first office space inside the same building.

I will say that I am very blessed to have some close friends and family that were so supportive of this project. I can't thank them enough.

Here are some pictures of our first wind turbine as it was being constructed in the warehouse. That's me on the right. Like I've said, the best feeling is seeing your hard work and planning finally come together. This wind turbine was actually designed as

a diaphragm that fills with air, which pressurizes a line that runs along the bottom of a lake to aerate the water. It was really nice seeing this monster spin for the first time and bubble up toward the surface.

This never would have been possible without the help and dependability of friends and family. Above, you can see my uncle Mark, my grandpa Harry, and my best friend/business partner, Jacob. This first project was a great learning experience for us. Each person brought his own knowledge and skill set to the situation. We quickly learned that safety is a key aspect in this type of industry, where you get to play with big machines.

Above we're adding the finishing touches to the turbine before it became active.

After our first official job, we began gaining lots of attention from large companies. The picture below was taken a few weeks later on one of our first business trips. It was one of the largest concept energy projects in North America at more than 11 megawatts. We had quickly entered into the big leagues.

Hopefully this background has helped you to better see how things progressed and how I started out. You can do the same. Take note of some of the ways I went about accomplishing my dreams. I suggest applying these concepts to your own projects and ideas. There's only one way to figure out if your idea is going to be a success: try it and give it your best when you do.

4
You Call That…
Success?

Everyone defines success differently; that's why it's a tricky subject to speak about. Most people define success as having lots of money, power, or fame. It's not any of that. These can very well be the fruits of your success, but it's not always so.

Success can be defined as achieving an aim or purpose. I can agree with this, but it was upsetting to see that the next three definitions listed had to do with prosperity or wealth. Chances are, if you're a self-motivated, ambitious, or entrepreneurial-minded person, then you will most likely have a looser version of this word. I say this because we see every small achievement as a major accomplishment. Oftentimes what we are trying to do has never been done before in the manner we are trying to do it in. Just a side word of advice: keep the glass half full, because tough times will come, but dedication is what will see you through.

I choose to define success as the point when you are satisfied with the fruits of your labor. Typically, you are satisfied when you achieve what you set out to do in the first place. In today's society, it's easy to get fame and wealth confused with success.

Here is an example of success that is probably one of the most humble and simple definitions of it. I would like to give some recognition to a man who has had a tremendous influence on my life. He wasn't rich and he wasn't famous, but he was successful. I am talking about my grandfather.

He spent his early life very poor. His parents did almost anything to get by. When he was around fourteen he took a full-time job to help feed his younger siblings. As he grew older, he became a main supporter of his family. When he became of age, he joined the military. After several years of military service as a demolitions expert and paratrooper in the Korean War, he came back to civilian life to start a business. He was able to start his own welding supply company servicing the southern United States. One day he received a call to do some private work for the state of New York. After a few months, he had successfully built the first trash truck that we know of today. He then flew back home to continue his business and expand to be one of the largest fire extinguisher companies in the South. During all of this, he was an accomplished used vehicle dealer, selling everything from planes to fire trucks. These were his passions. He did them and did them well.

He didn't believe in ripping people off or overcharging. He wanted to do an honest job. He would never put his name on something if he couldn't absolutely certify that everything was perfect.

My grandfather was able to accomplish some great feats during his life. Overcoming all these obstacles was challenging, especially considering where he came from. It required perseverance. You need to envision what you want, and then don't stop for anything until you get it. He always would tell my brothers and me that there is always a way to accomplish something.

He said, "I grew up on Tough Street. You know where I lived? I lived all the way at the end of the street after the last house. I was after the last house, in the woods, with my tent."

He would always tell me this when we were working on the farm and would come across a problem that seemed too complicated to overcome. Then we would sit back and consider our options. We always found a way out. From then on, I never let myself get backed into a corner in a tough situation.

These are just examples of the small struggles or bumps that will happen along the way to achieving your end goal. I believe the most lethal thing for entrepreneurs is themselves. I've realized that I can get so invested in a project that the only thing I will accept is the finished product that I've envisioned. The key to not burning out is to celebrate every achievement. When I started my clothing brand, I celebrated the success of opening a website. I celebrated the success of advertising on Google and

Facebook. I celebrated the success of selling my first piece of clothing on the East Coast. Every car my grandfather sold, he celebrated that achievement. Every project his company completed for a client, they celebrated. The most important thing to do in order to keep your own morale up is to celebrate and appreciate the small things.

Let me ask you this. How many people have achieved the same things you have? How many people did I know at the time that could successfully run their own website, company, store, etc.? Your answers should be very few or none at all. I didn't know anyone under thirty years old who had accomplished the same things I set out to do at fifteen. If there are lots of people who have done what you are trying to do, then you're not thinking outside of the box enough. Celebrate every step of the process! When you get your first meeting with a potential investor or client, that's a big deal. Be happy! It's OK to let people know.

It's healthy to think about what sets you apart. Always stay motivated. Everyone does it differently. Remember what sets you apart from everyone else. You want to be a difference maker and a world changer. If you tell yourself this enough, you'll start to believe it. When times get tough because you have declined in the rate of successes you are having, focus on where you're going. It's just like when we were younger and you were told to "keep your eyes on the prize." It applies here too. Keep your attention on where you want to be, and make every decision so you can arrive there.

The journey is half the fun. As you travel along the way to achieving your potential, enjoy the ride. You will meet many new faces and have lots of new experiences. Cherish moments like these. These things will happen as you make your way toward your goal.

5
The F Word: Failure

Failure. All right, now that my most hated word is out there, we can start the chapter. Failure is one of the hardest things to learn to accept, but it has to be done. In order to be able to move past this point, you have to realize that whatever you tried to accomplish is not going to happen just yet.

I prefer to think of these stages as — you guessed it — works in progress. For me, if I have something that I am passionate enough about, you can bet that I am going to see it through. It doesn't matter to me how many times I fail doing it. I will try until I have exhausted every one of my resources.

This is where my most important advice comes into play. You must have faith in yourself and your ideas, because a lot of the time you will be the only one who does. I have faced adversity my whole life trying to fight this uphill battle. Very rarely will this be an easy fight. Look at Steve Jobs—he had a revolutionary invention, but it took years of dedication to bring it into existence. Look at Apple now. You have to be your biggest fan.

Here, I'll share some stories about my entrepreneurial journey. This first story isn't about failure; it's about the most common way to achieve failure. By now you have read about how I started the small jewelry business that ended up being its own clothing brand. Imagine being a fourteen-year-old going on fifteen just entering high school as a freshman. The big kids always called us "fresh-meat." As if I didn't already feel intimidated. Remember, this was the starting point of my business. I was working hours each night creating new pages for the website, on top of homework and football practice after class. Time was a necessity.

Now, as a new kid in high school who was trying to start his own business, I was talked about a lot. I would say I became popular, but it wasn't always good things. Other students were asking questions about every aspect of the business. Most of my friends tended to be like my cheerleaders. I was very thankful to have classmates that had my back.

But as Newton always said, for every action there is an equal and opposite reaction. There seemed to be just as many people who told me I couldn't do it and I wouldn't amount to be anything. I remember having a friend of mine tell an adult that I was trying to start a business, and I received nothing but laughs and a "we'll see." I have to say that as much as these comments bothered my young teenage self, they were the best thing that ever happened to me.

This is the most important thing about accepting these comments: don't. You have to be the source of your motivation. You are the only one who knows the future of your idea or business. Whenever someone said things like this to me, I would take it and turn it in to even more motivation. My response was always, "We'll see; just watch." I would then add them to a mental list of people I wanted to prove wrong.

This negativity, which admittedly was thrown at me by very few, was just what I needed to help drive my ideas forward. I wanted to show people that I could amount to something. The whole time I kept my head up. It's hard to stay positive when you have bumps along the way, but it's never impossible.

Four years later. It's my senior year of high school. There was a particular person who had been one of the biggest criticizers and nonsupporters of my business throughout high school. His goal was to bring me down any way possible. That person ended up apologizing and asking me for a job. I was unable to give him a job, but that was a very rewarding feelings. To have someone say that, who had been so negative all along. This is what I mean: the day when your idea becomes something is the day your haters will change also.

I looked forward to days like these as a young fourteen-year-old trying to make something for himself. I knew days like these would come. It all came down to knowing where my idea would end up. I knew my potential. You are the only one who knows how to get there, and no one else can do it for you.

You're probably wondering what this has to do with failure. It has everything to do with failure. When starting something new, you are the driving force behind it. If you want it bad enough, you will succeed. It may not happen exactly how you wanted it, but there is a reason everything goes the way it does.

The easiest example of failure can be related to sports, or in my case football. Easy enough—it's pretty much just pass-fail, which I always thought was easier. When I used to work in college football, we would have intense workouts and practices for the players designed to test not only physical strength but mental strength also.

Now take a moment and place yourself in the shoes of a running back. When you look across the line at your opponent, you see a big scary linebacker, right? Wrong—you've already lost this play, and it hasn't even started yet. Now you ask, how on earth did I lose already? You were beaten mentally, my friend. You saw your challenge, and you gave him more credit than he's worth. In reality, you both match up about equally in physical strength. But this isn't always an even match-up scenario. You will never face the same problem where you can handle it the exact same way twice. You were so focused on how scary he was that you forgot there are other ways of beating this guy for one play. Agility is your ticket here. Beat him with speed and dynamic footing. This is the type of solution that self-starters, entrepreneurs, and ambitious people need to have.

Remember your resources and what you're good at, then put them to work. Not everyone can do what you do; otherwise, everyone would be trying to be like you.

It's situations like these that coaches try to prepare their players and fellow coaching staff for every day. You cannot allow yourself to be mentally beat. You may have heard sayings from coaches such as, "It's only 10 percent physical; the rest is all in your head," "Ninety percent mental," and "Don't beat yourself." I heard these sayings about every day for seven years. This is one of the most truthful lessons I can bring from athletics. It may have taken seven years to learn it, but I don't look at a problem and judge it by its strengths. I blink and see its weaknesses. Not everyone can do this. This has been a very valuable and unique skill that has helped me in all aspects of life, not just professionally.

Picture yourself as the running back again. You look across the line and see what appears to be a big, scary guy, but wait—he's bent over with his hands on his knees. He's trying to take a break and get some air. Now you see a weakness. He's tired. Since he is tired, he will have a slow reaction time. You now know you can beat him by using your footwork and speed.

The linebacker is like the bumps you face along the way. These bumps include everything from negative people to investors denying your proposal. Trust me, I've had the latter happen plenty of times. I may think my idea is the best thing since sliced bread, but they don't. Sometimes you simply need to be able to explain your plans more thoroughly. We see our ideas plainly, because they are *our* ideas. We know what we were thinking, but it can be hard for others to see our thoughts.

This leads me back to failure. So what is it?

Failure is not when someone says your idea is stupid.
Failure is not when someone says you'll never make it.
Failure is not when someone denies your investment proposal.
Failure is not when your patent isn't approved.
Failure is not when you didn't make that sale.
Failure is not being unsure of where to go next with your plan or idea.
Failure is not when you decide to wait on your project or idea to pursue another.

Failure IS when adversity strikes and you lose. In other words, failure is when you choose to give up. Plain and simple.

Failure is not bad. But never choose failure unless you have absolutely exhausted every resource in order to pursue your dream. Sometimes the best way to move on from one idea to another is to accept it as a failure.
When I was a kid, my dad would always tell me how Michael Jordan failed many times before he became the star we know today. He would tell me how he didn't make the cut in high school and about all the try-outs that didn't go the way he wished. He

kept driving toward his goal no matter what. He didn't let any negative comments stop him from doing what he envisioned. Throughout my childhood, my dad reminded me of this. Whether it pertained to sports or academics, it didn't matter. He made me realize that failure happens to everyone. What makes people different is how they act when failure strikes. Are you going to quit? I sure hope not.

Now that fear of failure is out of the way, here are some ways you can overcome and avoid it. The biggest problem with pursuing good ideas is that motivation doesn't seem to always be a natural resource. For people like you and me, we need to find it and find it quick. Time flies, and before you know it, you've spent three months working about forty-five hours per week after your full-time job with hardly any sleep. The day you start to analyze everything that has occurred is the day you start to realize you haven't gotten much out of your work. There are times when this realization is tough. It can be a good and a bad thing. The trick is to stay positive and always view the cup as half full. Of course, it is a good thing to realize the reality of where your business is at, but just don't overthink it. Compared to everyone else, you're well ahead of the game. How many people do you know who work another full-time job for free doing something that they hope will change the world? Not many. Stay positive and focus on the future and its endless possibilities.

I want to share with you some tips for dealing with negative thoughts and situations. At the end of the day, you need to know yourself. If you don't already, introduce you to yourself, because you're going to make a new friend. It's easy to convince yourself that all of your hard work is going to waste. After the first couple months it can get boring, because you've lost motivation to continue your work. This is when adversity sets in. Adversity is when you realize how far you have left to go and how hard it is going to be. Instead, realize how far you have come. I mentioned earlier the importance of celebrating every point along the journey. I wasn't kidding. Your morale is the only thing keeping your dream afloat. Fuel it.

This whole chapter has been about placing failure in a positive light. Don't let it turn into some life-threatening ordeal. Remember what I said about keeping a "glass half full" mentality? The solution is to be willing and open to change.

One of the most important life lessons I learned was in high school and later influenced in college football. In high school I was a below-average-sized linebacker. I wasn't the best; I didn't have every play memorized. What I actually enjoyed most was knowing what our coach anticipated and then seeing how the play followed through. I loved watching how preparedness influenced the play. But most importantly, I learned how to be successful. There were plays where our massive, strong, athletic linebacker, who was way better than I was, would decide to do something on his own. This can be a risky move on the player's part, because if you mess up, then you're going to become an expert on sprinting...after practice. There were times when the play wouldn't go the way the coach had planned, mostly because the player didn't do his job. This tended to continue, and more failure followed suit, until the moment came when the coach found someone else for the job. My thoughts were always the same: "Why didn't you do your job?" Most of the time the play failed because someone chose to do something other than the game plan. This was a recurring thing among certain athletes. Why would someone choose not to do his job?

I learned that I needed to be coachable. This has come up in every job I have ever had. Whether an employer or employee has noticed or not, you have to be willing to learn and adapt to your new environment. If the player messes up, he messes up. Then the coach does what he does best and coaches the player on the right way to do things. If the player continues to do the wrong thing on purpose, he is being uncoachable. This can ensure failure.

Imagine this conversation:

Me: "Do you ever stop being educated?"

The other guy: "Yes, Cooper, because I just graduated and I'm not going to go to school anymore."

Me: "Oh really. I forgot learning is only done in classrooms. So you're never going to learn new things to advance your knowledge and skill set to become successful? That makes a lot of sense."

Believe it or not, I have met a plethora of people with this mentality. To people like you and me, this can seem depressing. Everyone has so much potential—don't throw yours away. It doesn't matter what degrees you have, or how many degrees you have. You can learn anywhere. I always refer to this as "being coachable." Not many people are used to this term, so it gives me a chance to encourage my coworkers.

I am always thankful when I have a situation that brings a definite outcome. What I mean here is when a situation brings closure. For example, when you present an idea to investors and they accept or reject your idea. Either way the situation flows, good or bad, is closure. If something good comes from this meeting, then I learn what to keep doing. If the outcome isn't so great, it isn't a failure. It's a learning opportunity.

There are always blessings in disguise. I strongly believe that everything happens for a reason. We may not see it right now or even a few years from now, but everything has a purpose.

I want to share some experiences about developing ideas in general. The first time I ever invented or designed anything was in my junior year of high school. It was a design for a piece of an electric car that could make the electrical components up to 220 percent more efficient with energy consumption. I met with my business mentor, who is a very successful man in various industries. We met at his house one afternoon after I left school. I came in and sat at his dining room table. This was the first time I had ever pitched an idea in my life. I was scared to death, even though he was a close friend.

There I began my spiel, which seemed to turn more into a rant. An hour and a half later, we began to converse more on the subject. Even though we didn't end up building the car, I learned something from this situation. I learned the first step in being an entrepreneur: get your idea together. I was so scattered that I couldn't keep my thoughts together. In my case I also learned how to keep someone's attention. I learned what to say and what not to say to business leaders. Just for your own personal information, keep it short and sweet. Don't ramble like I did. Keep intriguing them.

Have you ever heard of an elevator speech? It's a saying for when you meet someone in an elevator and he or she asks you about yourself. You should be able to give them a quick thirty- to sixty-second recap of who you are. The goal is to create enough interest that the other person wants to give you his or her business card. The same premise applies to ideas and proposals. You want to keep your spiel to about ninety seconds and really highlight the possibilities of your idea and its uniqueness. The ultimate purpose is to make people want more and hopefully invest in this business. This was something that eventually happened, and I learned something new each and every step along the way. I wouldn't be where I am today if I didn't improve each time.

Keep learning and never failing.

6
The Equation for Success

I sure hope that the mention of an equation didn't scare you. Don't worry, it's not too complicated. It is simple enough that it just might save your project.

You can thank my physics background for the equation. I sure hope you haven't lost familiarity with Newton's laws just yet. Now the laws of physics are conceptual, so we are going to think about business conceptually in order to view our idea in a different light. I have heard many ideas about business being thought of as an equation and this is the best understanding that I could develop and expand.

So picture this: you have a million-dollar idea. This thing is sitting there, and you have no idea what to do with it to get it off the ground. To make it clear, you have a rather large idea and you need to figure out how much drive you need behind it in order to launch it to success.

So here's the equation to success right here: F=MA. Look familiar? I hope it does, because it's basic physics. If not, no worries; allow me to explain. Everything that has to do with force in general is based off of this equation. F represents force, which is the measured amount of strength the object has. M stands for mass, which is the certain weight an object holds. And lastly, we have A, which stands for acceleration. Acceleration is a measured rate of increase.

Now, let's take a look at the properties within this equation. On the left side, we have a single variable, so we can conclude that it is neither increasing nor decreasing. On the right side, you see we have a multiplication problem that resolves to equal the left side. So you can see we have a one-sided problem here with a simple multiplier. Keep in mind that multiplication is the fastest growing function of the simple functions. Keep watching.

Let's pause here for a second. You're probably wondering, "Cooper, where are you going with this? Where are your numbers going to come from?" Just hold on with me. We are about to do some conceptual math here by redefining what these variables stand for. For all you math guys, there is calculator needed.

Back to step one. What is the first thing we begin with when we want to start something new? Hopefully you start with an idea and continue from there. Now that we have decided on an idea, we can call this our Mass (M). Now in order to solve an equation, we need to eliminate all other variables but one. This leaves us with either Force or Acceleration. We can find the value for Acceleration by looking within ourselves and deciding how bad we want this to succeed. Therefore, since our drive is directly related to our motivation, then A is equal to our motivation. Now let's zoom out.

We went from F=MA to F= (idea)(motivation). Remember the property of multiplication? Remember how quickly the solution of multiplication can grow? For example: 4=2x2, 6=2x3, 12=4x3, etc. If one variable is increased—even by just one—it can drastically increase your outcome. This is exactly what we want.

The equation looks like this in action. Once you have your idea, the better you can refine and revolutionize your idea or project, and the higher the outcome will be. As for your motivation, that's up to you. When you have an idea, you're the only one who has that exact idea. You can tell me about your idea all day long, but I will never have the same motivation that you do for it. It exists in your head; you know everything about it, including its possibilities. The motivation factor is controlled by you alone. I hope that if you're willing to even consider taking your idea farther that you support it 100 percent. You are the constant in this equation, and your drive must remain constant as well.

All right, so we've tackled the fun part. And now you say, "Cooper, we've just confused ourselves five times trying to use imaginary numbers. What does this all mean?" I will tell you exactly what it means.

Everyone has ideas, right? Ideas are your mass, or M. The opposite side of the equation houses your force, otherwise represented as F, which stands for your potential impact. So now you have F=M. If you don't have the dedication and motivation (which is represented by A), then your idea will go absolutely nowhere: Mx0=0.

The point is that we are wired differently than most people. Most people are all talk and no relentlessness. They give up at the first sign of a struggle. Don't let adversity win without fighting.

Entrepreneurs, inventors, and innovators have the only quality that can't be taught or learned. Rather, it's found within yourself. That's the drive and motivation to dream and do big.

7

The War on Change

I chose to interrupt the original flow of the book to bring to light a question that you will begin to ask yourself soon enough. As you seek to go out and develop the world for the better, you are often going to run into people that refuse to accept it. You can have all of the information, college professors, and PhD's backing up your case and they still won't "believe you". Growing up in the South, we come to call these people "hard-headed" or as my grandfather always put it "bull-headed". Their heads are so thickly engrained with how things have always been done that a change in the system would affect their daily routine more than they could handle.

We also call this being closed-minded. For the record, we are 100% open-minded individuals. We are actually probably the most open-minded individuals. We are the ones that seek the necessary change, and we need open-minded people in order to effectively implement our concepts.

I have often heard the response to change being, "Don't fix it if it ain't broke". Hidden within this very Southern saying is something that actually leads me to a very good point. Is the person that said this statement the one who is creating the change or are they the one who is receiving the change? It doesn't sound like a very encouraging statement for change now does it? Because it is not.

Why does it take businesses so long to make routine changes? Not every employee is going to see the reason why.

Think of it from your perspective now. You are an innovator, inventor, or entrepreneur. You are seeking to develop and implement change. This is especially hard to do when dealing with people who have never seen a perspective other than theirs. People are naturally afraid of change, because they tend to be comfortable with where they currently are. It is often too hard for people to picture things in a different light like the way you see them.

These different perspectives are known as paradigms. Paradigms are the way that individuals perceive, interpret, and retain the information that the world gives them. It's not exactly saying that the person is not educated enough to realize change from another perspective. They may have never seen a certain change within their industry from another industry's perspective.

Allow me to give an example. Alternative energy manufacturers and developers have been building wind turbines for a long time now. It's technology that has been in use for years. I may bring a new idea to the table one day. I want to create a wind turbine that pumps air to aerate a body of water for farming purposes. So, I go speak with the engineering team at our facilities, which results in a negative answer due to the fact that it's too much trouble or not our field. Excuse me. If all you do is seek to manufacture wind turbines, you're business will soon die out. There has to be room for innovation. The engineering team has failed to realize the possibilities from all sides of the project. They wanted to stick to what's comfortable for them. They are used to generating electricity with wind, not using pressure built up from wind in order to pump air.

They didn't see the potential from the physics perspective. Technology similar to this has been around for years, and this remains solely for illustration purposes. As the wind rotates the wind turbine, it drives a piston up and down inside of a shaft. As the piston is driven upwards, it pressurizes air into a diaphragm that releases the air through a pressurized tube that runs into various areas within the body of water. Once the rotational force of the wind overcomes the force of the water that remains above the depth of the hose, then it will work.

I understand that this may not have made sense to everyone reading this. Do you know why? Because we have our own unique paradigms. There aren't lots of people that I assume are physicists reading this right now. That's perfectly fine, but you're now open to the idea. I have actually assembled one of these before through one of our companies, Solaire Energy

Group. The engineers in this example were electrical engineers. I'm not saying that they don't understand physics concepts, because I know they do. Pertaining to the argument, it typically tends to be those who have been in particular field for a long period of time are the ones that place barriers to change. They have done things a certain way for so long, that they don't want to try something new. In this example it was not only the engineers that had a barrier to change, but the business leaders. The business leaders did not see the potential in creating a new product. There is a market for this item. A specific market, but a market nonetheless.

I hope that this example serves as a good illustration as to how barriers of change are created and recognized. You may wonder, "How do I overcome a barrier to change?" That's a question people have been studying for years.

In my personal experience it will take lots of hard work. Often times you will not be able to change a person's views. What I have done in the past was to get as many experts on my side as possible. I have gone to leaders of different companies and industries. Most often I have driven to Universities and walked into an engineering or business school. I sit down and talk with professors about the concepts, and I get the expert approval and backing to my ides. It may sound crazy to do something like this, but all they can do is tell you "No" or "Sorry, I can't help you". A small price to pay, to chase your dreams.

8

Discovering Innovation

Sound familiar? Maybe not. This is the slogan of the second company I started, which I carried over into the third. I put lots of thought into this motto. Before I created something life-changing, I needed to define what I wanted to accomplish as a company. My goal for Aurelia Enterprises — now called Cooper Wade Enterprises — was to fund projects of our own as well as startups in our specific focus areas. I wanted our motto to exemplify who we were.

Discovery represents something new. Discovery is something that changes industry from that point on. I wanted to be the one who supported discoveries. My dream was to change the world with my creativity.

Innovation is a change. It's a change in society that improves on or makes current means more efficient. I didn't want to be innovation; I wanted to discover it. I wanted to redefine it. I wanted innovation to be in the palm of my hand, ready to give to the world.

Discovering Innovation is where you implement change. I wanted to be a part of change in the world. Innovation is improving upon a current industry. I wanted to create new industries and markets, and this is still my goal. Take Steve Jobs and Apple, for example. He revolutionized the phone industry. Apple not only improved on existing products, but created a need for their product. They created a new market and a new industry for smartphones.

So you're probably thinking, how do you come up with ideas like these? There isn't a set method to changing the world. If there was, everyone would do it. Actually, I take that back—there are lots of unmotivated people out there. Everyone has had an idea for improvement at some point or another. Not many people are driven to make that idea a reality. It's hard to get motivation. Not many people know how to do it.

I'll tell you how I motivated myself. I wanted to be successful one day, so I started researching people who were already successful. Luckily, I had a good family friend who also became my mentor. I want to be able to share with you some of the things he did for me.

This man was a very humble gentleman who was very successful in the oil industry. I made it very clear where I wanted to lead my life, and he did everything to help influence and guide my business ambitions. Every couple of months he would send articles, books, some kind of memorabilia, or stories telling me about successful people.

Now, absolutely no one can tell you what to invent and how to make lots of money by just handing you the blueprints and doing the work for you. They're stupid if they do.

I think he knew exactly what he was doing all along. He was motivating me. I didn't realize till years later in college. I would sit and read each one of those books. There were some on men like Richard Branson, Michael Oher, and many other extremely successful people. He and his wife even introduced me to some of their friends in various fields. Needless to say, I was very blessed with the experiences. Through reading about and meeting these people, I was inspired. These experiences planted a seed of motivation that was fertilized every time this occurred.

I saw what these people were able to accomplish, and I wanted the same thing. My dream was to change the world. I have had many ideas of how I would do that in the past eight years, and I'm still working. My motivation hasn't left, and at this point never will. I set my vision with the end in mind, and I'm not going to let anything stop me.

I want you to be able to see what I envisioned by hearing my story. I hope you want to grab ahold of what your dream is. Do what is necessary to accomplish it.

Motivation is the first thing that can kill a wonderful idea. Don't waste time drawing and writing it out if you don't have the will to see it through. It's all in your head. Don't listen to negativity. Don't listen to a lazy mind. And simply, don't overthink it. Just keep your composure and focus on the endgame.

Picturing the best possible outcome is a great way to get motivated. I always try to imagine where this idea could lead me, and then I plan out the steps to point B, then C, then D, and all the way to Z. Find your big goal and then choose small ones along the way. The small ones are what are going to get you there. They keep the motivation going. Without the small successes — or the lack of recognition thereof — it can be pretty hard running on empty in motivation.

So now that you're ready to take on the world and quite possibly the universe, we need to get some ideas flowing. Getting the creative juices flowing can be different for everyone. Some people like to stimulate thought by listening to music, taking a hike, or depriving yourself of oxygen in your backyard pool. Now, before you start to question my sanity or ask if that was a typo, allow me to explain. There actually is a man who uses this technique combined with a few others to stimulate creative thinking. As unorthodox as his method sounds, he is actually one of the most successful inventors to ever live. He is from China and currently holds over three thousand patents for various inventions. Talk about one very creative person. The good news about this gentleman is that he knows himself. He knows how his mind works. He has figured out what inspires him, and he does it. It isn't exactly a safe way of doing it, but he has the concept.

Here's what gets me motivated. (I tend to be a little safer about it.) I listen to music while I'm working on a project or just relaxing on my balcony. It's a good way to stimulate brain function. Another thing I like to do is go to a place that is inspiring. For me, it's the beach. For someone across country, it could be snowcapped mountains or the Grand Canyon. Just simply sitting on a beach is inspirational for me. I look at the waves and imagine everything that going on the world. I also like to hike or walk around the city and just admire the buildings or landscape. That's probably the Arkansas side of me coming out, but I think you get the picture.

So now that you're motivated, you need to be dedicated. Dedication comes after motivation. This is when you make the decision to go all in. This is the commitment you make to yourself—or possibly others—when you begin this process. It's as simple as that. Well, the definition is simple, but putting it to action can take some work if a lot of things demand your attention. It can mean not going out with friends on a Friday night. It can keep you from doing a lot of things. But that's the difference between you and me versus everyone else. A lot of people don't have the dedication, because they were never motivated in the first place. What can it hurt? You only have one life, right? Might as well change the world for the better while you're here.

So at this very moment you are an extremely motivated person, who has vast amounts of dedication, and who is also ready for me to move on. Now we can finally continue discussing the creative stimulation. Perhaps you want to know where you can go on Amazon to order preprocessed ideas and have them sent to your house with free two-day shipping. Man, would that be nice. I wish I could just Google search ideas and print one out and make millions off of it. That'll be the day. Thinking of these things is hard work.

In fact, most of your ideas will come when you're not even trying to be creative. Most of them will happen as you go about daily life doing your routine habits. Maybe you'll realize the way you've always done it takes too much time. For example, a tall spouse has placed something on top the cabinets. Her shorter husband comes home and can't reach it. Thus, the stool is born! It's amazing. The creativity is unreal. They probably didn't even realize what they did either.

Then, a week later, Uncle Johnny comes over for dinner and accidentally breaks the stool. He thinks to himself, "I wish I could extend my arm…" Uncle Johnny goes home later that night and designs a metal shaft with a hook on one end and a handle on the other fashioned out of old soup cans. Thus, the high shelf grabber is born. Uncle Johnny became a millionaire shortly after. This is an exaggerated illustration, but it serves as a good example of how ideas are born. Most of them will happen through an experience like this one.

You can ask questions to help guide your thinking. This plays along with innovating based on an experience, where you find an easier way to do something without actually searching for it. Except this time, you are consciously looking for ways to improve. How can the normal processes be radically changed to become more efficient or productive? Look for areas mistakes tend to occur. Look for areas that take too much time for what it's worth. Once you find your problem, begin to migrate toward a solution. This is when you start asking "how?" Actually, during this whole process you ask how, because you're always developing and always expanding. Start with one idea and keep running with it. Sometimes you'll realize that the problem you looked to solve accidentally led you to another, completely different, solution.

Now, experiential innovation is not something that happens every day. It requires lots of patience to wait to run into a problem that needs fixing. That's a necessity that runs in low supply for me, and there are plenty of other things that usually demand my patience.

I try to use a little more proactive way to spark thought. I think about the direction that the world is moving in: What are some current political/environmental issues? What are some current consumer trends? How are certain products changing? For example, in recent years consumers have migrated away from using paper. Another change I have noticed is an increase in research and development for alternative energy. Lots of research in the transportation industry is taking place. Also, based on newly released devices, everything is starting to become integrated together. I mean, my fridge can be accessed from an application on my phone. From these observations, I actually designed a component for an operating system in electric cars that allows it to increase its range/efficiency up to 250 percent. This is just an example of how I did it. Give it a try:

What are recent products that have gained attention from consumers?

What direction are people going in for the future?

Are there any political issues that hint at what the future could bring?

Do any of the three questions above leave a space for a future innovation? In other words, can you anticipate any future advancements?

What kinds of change do you foresee?

How can I solve a potential issue in any of the areas I have specified?

What can I do to develop a product or service for these areas?

Your answers to the questions above should result in a possible direction for you to move toward. Congratulations, because you have just started the creative process. But don't stop there! You have lots of work to do. Keep building on the idea. Start to ask questions like:

Can I expand the audience to apply to more people?

Could this product affect another industry?

Could I expand my product to be in its own market?

These questions will help you fine-tune your idea. Use tactics such as mind mapping, list making, comparison diagrams, etc. Ideas like these can also be used to create ideas and not just refine projects.

Mind mapping is a technique you probably used in grade school, but it still works. If you are not familiar with the process, allow me to explain. You take your idea or an industry you would to expand and place it in the middle of a piece of paper. Now you begin to think of all the factors that play a role in this project or idea. If you already have an idea of what you want to create, then use this to generate ways you can expand the application of your product. It's perfectly all right to put the most outrageous ideas on this diagram. Sometimes, if you give it some time, the idea isn't as crazy as it seemed. The same thing goes for simply trying to generate ideas in the first place. Start with an industry you at least halfway care about. Keep in mind, if you're not interested in the industry or the potential idea, then you may not want to venture off in that direction. You need to have some kind of emotional investment, because then you're more likely to succeed.

Hopefully you understand how this technique works. I'll explain it for all my visual minds reading this. When you place your topic in the middle of the page, draw a line moving away from the middle topic and write your new related subject at the end of the line. I draw a circle around every small topic as I develop. You keep branching off from every idea, and it ends up looking like a spider web. When you finish you can hopefully see your thought process as it evolved. Look back at it and see what seems possible and go for it. Develop your idea and see what happens.

I've used this process many times to help refine my ideas. It usually works. Sometimes the simplest of ways can yield the biggest results. There isn't some high-tech way of getting ideas I'm hiding from you, so don't worry.

I also love to make lists. I usually write different industries at the top of a page and put ideas below each industry that all relate. I then select an idea and expound on it by using a mind map or making a list of pros and cons. This is just a way that was successful for me. Everyone is different and everyone's brain functions differently. You aren't always going to get ideas from sitting at the beach like me; you might have to be in the car listening to music. We are all uniquely different.

It doesn't matter what level of education you have. You don't have to know everything about a topic in order to create something for it.

Albert Einstein once said, "Imagination is more valuable than knowledge."

One of the smartest men in the world placed imagination above knowledge. You can know everything about a topic and still lack creativity. Having an imagination is a commodity that very few people know how to access. If you can practice using your imagination, it can be one of the post powerful skills you possess. Think of business leaders — they need to be creative and imaginative to come up with new markets and decide how to enter them. Have you heard of the Imagineers? Take the Walt Disney Company, for example. They have a whole business department dedicated only to imagination.

Imagination and creativity is a commodity.
Practice it.
Develop it.
Then put a price on it and sell it.

9
Developing Your Idea

This is where the fun begins. Remember when I talked about celebrating the small achievements? Proceed to do so now. I'm not talking about throwing a party or baking yourself a cake, but sit back and recognize this moment. Pat yourself on the back. Tell a close friend. These things will help motivate you, because you're already farther than most people just by starting.

Deciding on your idea is a huge step. Now that you know what you want to achieve, you need to envision it. Take time to sit back and think about where this idea could go. Where it could be applied. Once you have gotten a snapshot in your mind of a possible end result for this ambition, go for it. Like I said, it's OK to dream a little bit. I mentioned some of this in the last chapter, but it's a concept that is recurring, and you need to keep it in the front of your mind.

After you pass out the party favors, you need to focus on how to expand your idea or project. Again, lists are fantastic here. For me, when I start thinking about my projects, I come up with so many possibilities in a short amount of time that if I don't write them down, I will forget them. Word to the wise: keep a journal near you at all times. I have two. I keep a book-sized journal in my briefcase or car and a pocket-sized one usually on my person. These are my go-to when I have an idea. I hate when I get a great idea and forget it moments later, so this is my solution. It may sound old school, but it works. The point is that it also works exceptionally well during the generating phase. Even if it seems like a bad or impossible idea, simply writing it down can lead to an amazing innovation further down the road.

During the development stage, you are all about refining your product or project. Let's start with products and then I'll review business plans, because they are very similar but contain different goals. Our goal is to arrive at a finished product where we can answer any possible question on it. The three main types of questions you need to answer are questions from the consumers, questions from the investors, and comparison questions. The consumers are the people who are going to fuel your business. Without them you have nothing. They are going to want to know why they should buy this amazing new item or how they can use it. For example:

Is it microwave safe?

Do I need batteries?

Can I connect my phone with it?

Your goal for these types of questions is to provide enough information so the customer can feel comfortable with buying your product. You want to instill confidence and trust in the employee. Make them feel like they are helping themselves by making this purchase.

Next, you need to focus on your potential investors. Investors tend to get a bad rap from various televisions shows. In reality they want you to succeed. They want to see an idea that will innovate and revolutionize the world. Most investors you will encounter have very precious time schedules, and it is very important that you focus during these meetings. I have faith that you will do just fine during the pitch, because if you care enough about your product and you've brought it this far, hopefully you will be prepared.

Essentially, what you are trying to do is present the evolutionary information to your investor. They will ask things like:

What makes this different from everything else that exists?

What is my potential for profit?

How much are you looking for and for what share of the company?

How can I benefit from this investment?

As you can see from these sample questions, the investor is typically focused on what is in it for them. They want to know why they should give you their money. Why do you deserve their attention and capital? This is the million-dollar question you need to answer.

The next type of question relates to comparisons, and these can be very similar if not the same as what you told the investors. These questions are going to be for the legal side of things. If you've invented something, they want to know how similar it is to everything else on the market at this moment. Here are some popular ones:

How did you get this idea?

Is it based on or does it utilize any existing inventions?

How is it better than anything else on the market?

Is there anything that is currently being researched related to this type of invention?

Is your design more efficient? And in which ways: finance, speed, production, etc.?

Can you show us how efficient your design is?

I hate to break it to you, but for most people, this is the hardest part of the developmental process. This is where all your fact-gathering and testing come into play. If you don't have much technical knowledge on your product, this could make or break you. This step is key in getting a patent. The Patent Office, your investors, or any company selling your product is going to want to know what's different about this design. It's best to have hard facts. The more you can tell them, the better off you're going to be.

I understand that not every product has to go into detail about testing and functionality. You may have developed a simple toy or kitchen utensil that requires little to no testing. In this case you would focus on researching marketability and the potential audience. When it comes to marketing and consumers, this is what will drive your product. You don't make money unless they buy it. Whether it's a simple product or not, this still needs to be a main focus.

So you say you want to start a business? If you have a product idea and followed the developmental process above, you have basically already started. Each type of question is conceptually the same. From a business standpoint, you need to decide on the service you're going to perform. There are different ways of going about this.

I view these different ways as having complex products, simple products, and services. There are many ways of trying to provide an outline for small businesses, but these are the three main ones that I have used as an entrepreneur. For starters, if you have a complex product in mind, then you may want to consider offering installation and repair services. If you have a simple product, such as one for merchandising, you might think about expanding your product line and opening your own retail store. Maybe you even want to manufacture your own simple products. Maybe your business is not based off of a product you created but it's simply to perform a specific service. For example, if you run a convenience store, you provide the service of selling other companies' products. On the other hand, there is another form of service, such as a landscaping company. They usually don't sell products but provide a specialized service of professional lawn and garden care. Each functionality evolves just a little differently.

For business plans you typically only have to worry about the consumers and your investors. The first order is to figure out who your audience is and what brings them to your line of business. You want to do some market research. Take a look at other businesses in your area that provide the same service or a similar one. Sample and use their services a time or two. Look at their reviews online and see what attracts their customers. Questions you can ask are:

How can I set myself apart from what already exists?

What do they do differently to attract their customer base?

Is their customer base primarily made up of return customers?

How can I change this industry, so when I enter, I can change the way business is done?

This last question is arguably the most important one to ask. From my perspective, I think changing the industry is good. People tend to like new trends within old businesses. If it's not done right, it can end badly. But as long as you go about it with the proper research, you can take almost any industry and change the way it functions. Not everyone has to do business the same way.

These guides are just rough outlines of the kind of things to anticipate. Like I said earlier, every idea is different; it all depends on you and your judgment. I have run into many roadblocks along the way, but that just gave me a chance to refine the product a bit. That's all this development stage is about, refining.

Allow me to walk you through my personal experiences of my various types of ideas. Over the years I have had all types of ideas. They've varied quite greatly, as many close friends and business partners can testify to. I have entered every industry from clothing to solar and even attempted the auto industry. Life can lead you to some unexpected areas.

I was lucky that I found an interest at a young age. I always was intrigued by energy and alternative forms. One concept that grasped my attention was the study of perpetual motion. Let me fill you in on the subject real fast. This is a concept that is quickly shot down by physicists like myself due to some basic laws of physics and energy, but I wanted to challenge it. You may not be able to have 100 percent perpetual motion, but who says you can't have a 99 percent efficient motion device? Now I understand you may be confused, so allow me to explain. Perpetual motion is a theory that once something starts to spin, it can keep spinning forever. This is technically impossible under normal Earth-like circumstances. I wanted to find a way that we could get as close to being 100 percent efficient as possible. This is the goal of every engineer and physicist alive, but I wanted to do it using the same concept. So I went to work.

Believe it or not, I started my studies in this subject when I was fifteen years old. I started by studying a man I heard about in school, Leonardo da Vinci. He once said, "O speculators about perpetual motion, how many vain chimeras have you created in the like quest? Go and take your place with the seekers after gold." He was comparing the criticizers of his work to people trying to seek riches from gold.

To him, their attempts to attack his work were as foolish as risking your life for gold. It made me wonder why one of the smartest men who ever lived would say this. I thought (and still do) that energy is the world's future. I wanted to find a way to make machines more efficient.

Anyway, I kept hard at studying numerous inventors' and scientists' works in these fields. I finally developed my own theorem based on other laws of physics. I showed it to some physics professors and teachers, as my idea seemed to prove true for the most part. As I set off to gain investors, I hit a dead end when I couldn't afford to build a prototype. I needed around $21,000 to construct the device for testing. As a small-scale version of my idea began testing, there was one theory that didn't hold true due to the circumstances. So my idea ended up not being as efficient as I had planned. I kept trying to refine it to also use things such as solar power and forms of polarized alternators. I kept trying—key words.

The problem with my design was that it was supported by theories, some of which assumed a little too much for investors to feel comfortable with. Unfortunately I didn't get to build a full-scale functioning car.

Now look at how I went about this. I started the process by having knowledge of the industry I was stepping into. The first thing anyone is going to want to know is how well you know your topic. You should have some sort of credibility, whether it's an expert opinion, educational background, or previous work experience. In this experience, I had physicists and other engineers help write the plans and verify that what I was actually saying was in fact true. Knowing your field is important. Keep in mind, what makes you an expert?

You can see that I also refined my idea along the way. When I realized my original idea didn't have enough energy being generated, then I went to alternate sources of energy. I expanded the way the car functioned so it was applicable to more environments and had access to more energy resources.

I didn't share this with you, but this idea also contained a business plan. Depending on the investor, I had created a car company that made cars specifically for these special modifications. I even went as far as lining up a car manufacturer that would build the car frames, body, interior, and key components for us. By the end of all of it, I had everything planned out to exactly where and how the car would be constructed. These companies were just waiting for the go-ahead.

The point is that I was prepared for any questions anyone might have. I had the market research. I had a marketing plan. This is exactly how you should go about new projects. Try to envision every possibility, even though you won't. It won't always go as planned, but try to be prepared.

Even though this idea didn't lead me to the success of being the owner of a massive car company, I gained lots of insight. Three years later, as you've heard by now, I started my alternative energy–based business. I carried my knowledge over into this field and continued my research. This business wasn't based around a specific product like the previous. Instead, we focused on services.

I wanted to continue in the energy business. I decided to install and service alternative energy devices. This wasn't an extremely hard task to go about considering Arkansas didn't have much business in this industry. We were the only company in this market within about two hundred miles. In this situation we didn't drastically modify the way business is done in the solar industry like I had mentioned in my "outline." We simply set out to provide a service to consumers who simply didn't have affordable access to it in the first place. Sometimes it can be as easy as that.

A helpful word of advice would be to stay up-to-date on current technologies within your industry, whether you have an idea, or are running your business, or even if you don't have either. Eventually you will. Industry knowledge will help you know where the technology is going. This s a very valuable attribute for a leader to have. Staying up-to-date is key, because it can give insight into possible new lines of business. This means more revenue.

You can even do like I did and choose something specific to research in your free time. I'm not saying you have to stay up late next to the coffeepot while reading dissertations, but this will allow your mind to continue to ponder ideas on the subject.

No matter which type of project you have in mind, sit back and ask as many questions as possible about it. Pick at your own idea. Try to find its weaknesses.

Have you ever heard of lateral thinking? This is a highly sought after skill for innovative people. This is a theory developed by a Mr. DeBono. His research is about taking one single idea and having one person view it from six different ways. In our situation, we want to see every side, such as marketing, manufacturing, accounting, leadership, etc. Look at it from as many relative ways as possible. Keep in mind, the goal is not to tear your idea apart but to enhance it using this process.

Throughout this whole process of refining, you will run into hard times where it can become a struggle to continue. You might even have to accept failure due to an unforeseeable aspect. No one gets everything right the first time. I started with a car design in mind, and as alternative energy played out over the following five years, I ended up with an alternative energy business. Failures will guide you to where you need to be. They are the moments where you sit back and have to make a change in order to keep on developing. A researcher by the name of Robert Sutton said that, "When there is less failure, there is less innovation." He is absolutely correct. Failure drives progress. It pushes you closer to success. Just remember to keep refining and keep improving your ideas, and one day it will fall into place. Everything is a learning opportunity.

10
Pause: Network

One of the best things you can do for yourself is something you can start working on right now. Think about where you want to be and how you want to get there. Who do you know that is successful? Think about how they got there. This can be anyone— you don't have to be a world changer to be successful.

So hopefully you have someone in mind. The next step is to go out of your way to have a conversation with this person. Try to get twenty minutes where you can ask him or her about their life and how they got to where they are today. The goal is to create a relationship with this person in the hopes that you can rely on him or her to help guide you with your ambitions.

This process is called networking. I want to stop here in the middle of the idea journey to let you in on this strategy. Networking is where you meet other people and keep in touch with them. They don't have to be successful or famous. Down the road these people can be great resources for you.

We all know someone who has said in reference to a successful individual, "I went to high school with that guy or girl" or "I grew up with them." Don't let this happen to you where you lose contact with someone. If at all possible, try to keep some connection.

You may come to rely on these random people you meet throughout your life. Place a value on every relationship, because they will come into play.

11
Where to Next?

So you have your great idea—now what? Where on earth do you go now? This is when people start to give up. This is when they fail. This is when they look at their situation and start telling themselves negative things. They start talking themselves out of moving forward by saying things like "This idea won't change anything," "I don't know what to do now," or "Other people are probably already working on this idea, and they're a lot smarter." Are you kidding me? People are always working on similar ideas. You'll never know what could have been if you don't try. Just because you have no idea on how or where to start your idea doesn't mean that you can't try. Those are horrible reasons to give up and accept failure.

These are the times when people tend to fail. They sit back and examine where they want to go and how they're going to get there. When they look at it, they scare themselves. Yes, there is going to be a lot of hard work, but that is what it takes. Hard work and sometimes unusual work is the only way your idea is going to make it.

Your three main goals at this step of the developmental stage are focus, functionality, and efficiency. You need to focus on your goal and not let anyone stop you. Then you will center your work around efficiency and functionality so you can get the best use out of your money.

We hear this term called "adversity" mentioned a lot. This is exactly when you start to see adversity. If you thought that refining the idea was hard, just wait till you deal with lawyers (no offense to lawyers; I was raised by one). Adversity is when you realize you're going to be fighting an uphill battle. Giving up is not an option. (Well, technically it is, but it's not one you're going to accept. You've made it this far.)

I have faced adversity many times. I realized in high school athletics what adversity really was. Anyone who has played football knows that feeling when the guy you have to stop is massive and all of a sudden you don't want to do this anymore, but it's your job to. You have to do it now, or else you get to have fun running for it.

There are a lot of things that can bring adversity throughout this process. If you're a young person trying to do these kinds of things, you're already in the middle of it. I'm twenty years old right now, and I'm still in the middle of it. Being fourteen years old and trying to start a clothing brand is not an easy task. Starting an alternative energy company when you've never worked for one is also not easy to do. It's also hard to sell shares of your new company when it's being run by a twenty-year-old.

People won't see what you see in it. They won't understand the potential of your ideas. There aren't many people in the world who are optimistic and see the glass as being half full. Out of the people that are optimistic, there are very few who are innovators or entrepreneurs. In fact, there are very few innovators and entrepreneurs in general, but if you're going to be a successful one, then you have to be optimistic.

For me, adversity usually came in respect to my age. And when I say in respect to my age, I mean no respect. Every person was already speculative because I was young. Age can put up a large barrier. I always had questions asked about my age when trying to fill out paperwork or get licenses. It only added to the satisfaction later on. As for alternative energy, I always had questions about my credentials. I would simply tell them about small jobs I had done here and there. There also weren't any other choices for solar energy providers in central Arkansas. Either way, people will find a way to be speculative. At every step it will occur. Just keep moving and ignore it. It's their own ignorance.

So where to begin next? There are different ways of going about ideas and projects from here. When you want to pursue selling your new idea, it tends to be a lot easier. But nonetheless you still go down a similar path. In order to figure out which way to go, you need to consider what you want. With some ideas you may have more success selling the rights to a large, established company; some ideas you're better off pursuing yourself. Use your discretion wisely.

So at this point you should be absolutely certain that you're not copying someone else's invention or creation. The last thing you want is to be working on something that's already been done, or even worse, break into patent laws.

The next step is to consider your resources. The reason I interrupted the flow of the chapters to include networking is because it is the single most important thing one can do. When you're approaching the point where you to go for it, you will need these people to get you through. You are not alone—most of the people who have fantastic ideas like you don't have the finances to bring them to fruition. It's also scary entering an industry that you don't have lots of experience in.

I would start by thinking about who your relevant resources could be. One suggestion would be fellow entrepreneurs, but those tend to be few and far between. It could be anyone in the industry, or an attorney, an accountant, or even your local small business office. (I am always cautious about small business offices, because I've visited some in the past and have had truly exceptional customer service and absolutely awful service.) The place I have found to be the most helpful were actually local universities. I would visit the relative departments to speak with professors and deans, and oftentimes they were more than willing to help. Take advantage of anyone who's willing to offer a hand, but make sure you can trust this person. You don't want anyone stealing your idea. Trust is important.

Your connections with these people will make your company great. The more input the better. Viewing your idea or product from multiple sides is important because it helps you to view any possible roadblocks for getting it off the ground.

Now to get started. If you wish to sell your idea, I can't really offer any advice rather than protecting your wants. This means a lawyer. Use some of your resources to figure out how much your idea is worth. The last thing you want to do is accept one hundred thousand dollars for an idea that's really worth one million dollars. You don't want that feeling in the pit of your stomach. It's not a good one. So be smart about it and know the company that you're dealing with. That's really all I can offer on that topic.

Entering the business world can be quite an experience. At this time you already have a good idea of your market and potential customers. Whether it's a new product or a service, you have to figure out the best way to offer it. Do you manufacture it yourself? Do you purchase space to open up your own shop? What about a website? There are many ways to establish your business.

Websites are always the easiest and most cost-effective way to start a business. For me, this has been my first solution every time. At fourteen years old, I started the jewelry and clothing company. The most logical place for me to start was by selling the product in person. I then moved to selling online. I reached a much larger crowd this way. Billions of people have access to the Internet, which is a lot more than the people who would drive down the road in front of your store. Use what will be most effective for you.

(My financial situation made the decision for me. It usually makes the decision for most people.)

The next most affordable and useful option was to purchase a trailer. It helped us expand, advertise, and sell our product. This was designed as a tailgating trailer outfitted with a HDTV, a stereo, a stockroom, and a cashier counter. The great thing about this new purchase was its efficiency. I could use it for much more than just hauling clothing; I could use it for marketing campaigns at local events and expos. The main focus when actually opening your business is efficiency: What is the solution that will get me the most for my money? How can I have the most effectiveness? How am I going to reach my customers?

Property is always something you want to focus on attaining, but if it isn't within your budget, then don't make it a priority. There have been many amazing businesses started from garages, home offices, and even barns. Everyone wants to look professional in the beginning, but it's not always possible to have the nicest vehicles, offices, or workshops. However, this is typically something that can really boost your company if you're in the services industry, because then your goal is to have professional office space. When I started my alternative energy company, I needed space to be able to run the business. There were lots of tools, equipment, machinery, and trucks that were needed. Luckily, I was able to use my resources. My relatives were in the agriculture and weapons industries and had plenty of space. So I simply asked if we could work out a deal to rent space.

After a few weeks, we had a functioning office space, warehouse, workshop, conference room, and garages for our trucks. We had a fantastic space to be able to conduct business. Professional office space makes a big difference when it comes to meeting with clients. If you want to claim to be a professional, you have to look like it.

12
Pouring the Foundation

Knowing where you want to be is one thing.

Planning for it is another.

Actually doing it is what makes us different from the rest of the world.

There are lots of dreamers in the world. Very few venture to figure out how they are going to accomplish their dream. During this step it's good to be realistic with yourself. Keep in mind that it's good to have very high goals, but it's good to have very low ones as well. The smaller goals are what will keep you going and driving for success.

This step is all about "putting boots on the ground," as they say. This when you go for it and actually begin to do business. I can't tell you exactly what to do at this point. I can offer some advice, but every situation is unique.

All I can suggest is to do your research. See what works best for you. Only you can determine what is necessary in order to fulfill your potential. Try to consult some professionals in the industry. See what others' advice is for your project.

Do what it takes in order to ensure your own success. For me, a website has always been my first step and most likely always will be. It's the most economical way to reach the largest audience in the world. In another business venture, purchasing trucks and warehouse space was the best idea. Determine what finances you have available and decide.

The most important thing is to keep the end in mind.

You are the only one who knows the true potential of your ideas.

As you make these purchases and decisions, know what needs to be done in order to achieve what you envision. Remember, there is no one way to do things in business. There are many ways to go about it.

If you truly have an impactful idea, the idea will eventually speak for itself. Don't dwell on making the wrong decision. Focus and make the best of whatever the situation may be — and where it can take you.

13
Leadership: Emerging Minds

There's no set list of qualities that a leader can possess. Everyone leads differently, and every company needs a different type of leader. Companies that have been around longer usually want someone who sticks to a certain type of management. New businesses or more innovative types of companies usually want leaders that are willing to take more risk and don't "go by the book." Sometimes, growing up, I wished some of my managers went "by the book." Like most people, I have worked for some great leaders, and I have worked for some that made me and my coworkers question how they had a job. The goal is to not be the latter.

In this section, I'll walk you through some skill sets and traits of great leaders that I noted from my personal experience. I have had the opportunity to personally work with many leaders, from the managerial level up to president and CEO. I have referred to them on which I should include. The following are some of the most important traits, we believe.

INNOVATIVE

I believe that an innovative leader is one that becomes an asset to the company. This kind of leader is one who actually brings the company forward. He or she is the one who comes up with innovative ideas to help your business. You can expand a company and create more franchises all day long, but there will come a day when you stop expanding like you once did. All of a sudden, your company isn't the only one serving fast-food burgers. If you want to truly grow a company, you have to be innovative.

As the most basic of examples, I had a jewelry business to start with. The only way I was going to continue the hype of my new company was to expand its product line. The only way I could do it affordably on our budget was to move into clothing. Clothing was cheap and very simple to enter into, because we had already established our business. Our goal was to generate even more cash flow by offering new merchandise. We ended up increasing sales by around 1100 percent with this change. A very simple change.

Every business needs innovation that's driven by innovators or at least those that encourage it among their employees. The larger the company, the trickier it is to do this, but there are ways around it.

I mentioned earlier in this book that there are statistics about innovative companies, gathered over the past ten years. We had two depressions in the early 2000s here in America. Most business leaders cut funding immediately to their research and development departments. Why would you do that? I'll tell you why. The logic with most companies is that research and development tends to be expendable. I'm not saying they view it as a lost cause, but that it is not a necessity, when in fact I would argue that it is the largest necessity. After the depression had ended, the companies that cut funding for research and development had lost 20 percent of their market value. That's huge. This department is what keeps your company moving. You don't want to be docile. You don't want to settle for being the largest and most successful company at what you do. If you stay docile for too long, someone else will step in and you'll be one step behind. Now this tactic isn't for everyone, so use it wisely, but it is applicable for most.

You may be wondering about service-focused companies. You may not have a research and development department, but you can still have meetings and brainstorm on how to expand. It's the concept that's important for you. It may take years to come up with a solution, but that solution could take you anywhere.

SHALLOW VERSUS DEEP

So reflect on past experiences. Did you notice the work ethic of your coworkers and managers? Think about what they dedicated their time to—this could be inside or outside of work.

Now, more importantly, consider your own.

How do you accomplish tasks on the job? Do you tend to do what you're told and nothing more? It's absolutely great if you help other coworkers finish their tasks or projects on time. But that's not what I'm talking about.

Have you done anything to improve your work environment? This can be almost anything. For example, it could be as easy as making something more convenient or safer to implementing a new stock inventory software that increases efficiency. These are the types of ideas you should want.

These types of ideas and projects can be referred to as "deep." This type of deeper work is what gets you recognized and promoted. Every company wants innovators; this is the simplest way to make it happen. Anytime you see how you can go above and beyond, take the opportunity.

Put yourself in the shoes of your leader or manager. Would you want your employees to go above and beyond to help perfect their role in the business? Obviously you would, because it then makes you look better as well. Your employees then also feel like their ideas are valuable. It works great all around.

Now shallow work is what difference makers want to avoid. We want to change and improve business. Shallow work is when you do what you have to get by. If this is how you go about doing your job, then plan on moving laterally or remaining stagnant, because successful businesses don't promote based on seniority. Work like the job you want. Think of problems that your boss may have and try to think of a solution. Let them hear your idea; even if they don't put your idea into action, it is still a plus for you. It implies that you care about your company.

It doesn't matter if you're in a leadership position or not. Deep work like this is highly sought after. Managers don't usually broadcast this subject, but it does work. Any way you can show that you are going above and beyond in your job is a plus for you.

So forget about just setting your mind to completing the tasks given to you and try to make some time to influence your company. You will not go unrecognized. This work stands out to lots of people and reflects on your personality and work ethic.

Like I have mentioned, it requires setting this as a goal for yourself and having enough motivation to achieve it. Know what you want and go for it.

COMMUNICATION AND DELEGATION

Without communication nothing can function properly. A good leader can communicate effectively. You are the one who must be able to communicate your ideas and plans clearly.

From an entrepreneur's perspective, this is a really important skill. You can have all the motivation you want, but without being able to communicate the idea, it could be fatal. I believe that communication and confidence go hand in hand. When you're presenting an idea to potential investors or customers, use the three Cs: you want to be clear, concise, and confident. It's important to be clear, because it allows your audience to understand your plans. It also helps to be concise. When selling an idea, you don't want to talk too much. Keep it short and sweet. Most importantly, you want to be confident. Speak with authority. Look confident. Feel confident. When you are confident on your speaking points, your audience will listen and be more inclined to follow your call to action. From an investor's standpoint, he or she will trust what you're saying more because you are confident in it.

The same works for leaders. Give your coworkers the faith to trust what you're saying. Never say too much; give them exactly what they need to hear. When you are confident, they will be confident.

INITIATIVE

Initiative is the will to start something. It is the source, where an idea begins. Everyone needs initiative to begin new projects. Initiative follows very closely with motivation. The difference between motivation and initiative is not a big one. Initiative is fueled by your motivation to keep an idea going. They flow hand in hand and keep each other going.

Leaders need to have initiative. Initiative toward everything. It's your job to incite change and ensure that it gets followed through. Without your initiative it would never get done. Your coworkers and employees see this and recognize it. If they see you leading by example, then they will follow and join in your efforts.

I've taken initiative my whole life. Every time I started a business or developed a new product or idea, I took initiative to get that product off the ground. There were times, like I've mentioned, that it seemed like I had everyone against me telling me I couldn't do it. I still took initiative when there weren't many who stood with me. It's hard to take initiative sometimes when it looks like the world is on your shoulders. This when true leadership shines. Now keep in mind that failure is always an option. But also keep in mind that when there is less failure, there is less innovation.

Innovation is the goal, and getting started takes some initiative. As an innovator, you are always the drive behind new ideas.

UNDERSTANDING

Now, being a leader means that your employees will often come to you with their ideas or problems. At the very least, simply be there to listen. More than half of your communication should be listening. Hear them out. Show you genuinely care.

The best thing you can do in any situation is to encourage. Understand where they are coming from. Try to put yourself in their shoes. It doesn't matter if they are going through personal struggles or having a work-related issue. Encourage them to overcome it. For work-related issues, try to find a solution. But most importantly, remember to try and connect with them on their level.

SUPPORTIVE

A leader isn't just a person set in place to run the show. They aren't just there to tell you what to do. This is the difference between managers and leaders. A leader will do more than simply ensuring that the environment is functioning properly. A leader looks out and is attentive for their employees.

In my eyes, and through my work experience, true leaders care about their employees' well-being. Yes, there are things that you can and can't talk about, but you should take an interest in your employees' lives. Make sure things are fine with them and their coworkers. Keeping up with your employees can help prevent drama in the workplace. In return, they will also know that you genuinely care about them and the company.

There are ways to lose respect by abusing your position. Take your authority seriously. You've heard this before, but don't let it go to your head. You don't want to prove your authority to your employees, because then they don't want to work with you. When this occurs they will not be as productive as you want.

The most important part of being supportive is having integrity and consistency. When you converse with your coworkers, keep your word; don't undermine their individual authority. For example, don't tell them something and then claim to have never said that when they repeat your words. This is a part of behaving consistently among all your employees. Your integrity is important, so take responsibility in circumstances like these. Now, I can't give you examples of every workplace situation that occurs. I gave you this as just one example that I have seen. It's your job to keep these processes in mind and use them in your own situations.

This leads us to the easiest way to lose respect. When you are helping employees, don't let them feel that you're favoring one over the other. This causes drama, which is not what we are about. So treat everyone the same and have integrity with your word.

BRING OTHERS UP

"Remember the little people."

If you've ever started showing potential or driving toward bigger and better things, you have probably heard this. It carries a lot of truth.

What I mean by this is to bring others up with you. People like you and me, we are driven individuals. Why not help bring other deserving people up along the way? Help your employees get promotions. Don't be one of those bosses on a power trip, refusing to help the little guys in fear that they could be his boss one day.

People will respect you more if you help them out too. I believe this should be a task for every manager. Keep an eye out for their aspirations and dreams. Try to find ways to help them meet upper management or apply for a new job or transfer. You will earn much respect when you look out for the little people.

RECOGNITION

What motivates people more than rewards? Think about the last time you received recognition or an award for something work related. How good did that make you feel? If you haven't had an experience like this, well, it feels pretty good. It can get pretty boring and seem meaningless sometimes when you're just a normal employee doing a laborious job. It isn't easy. Keep this in mind.

So consider some solutions. Find an appropriate way to recognize your employees. For example: awards for selling the most cars, assembling the most key chains, being employee of the month, and even awards based on years of service. Keep in mind the simplest and most cost-effective ways are more likely to get approved. Think of new awards you could start, or even celebrate birthdays with your employees. Recognition is a way for you to show appreciation. Try to do it as often as you can while still keeping it a special thing for your employees.

Appreciation is the goal of recognition. You want employees to feel appreciated. In return they will take pride in what they do. Do you know what happens when employees have pride? They become more successful and productive.

INTRINSIC MOTIVATION

Look back at the attributes and skills of a successful leader:
Innovative
Deep Work

Communication
Delegation
Initiative
Understanding
Bring Others Up
Supportive
Recognition
All these contribute to having one effect on your employees and coworkers. They become motivated.

This concept is called intrinsic motivation. This was studied by a social psychologist named Amabile. He focused his studies on how people can influence one another. The only way that you or anyone else is going to reach personal peak performance levels is if you have intrinsic motivation. Intrinsic motivation is something that is fueled from within. It's something that can only come from the person, not anything else.

Intrinsic motivation is the kind of motivation that you get when you're chasing some of your own ideas. In earlier chapters I mentioned how I motivated myself to chase after my dreams with each business idea. I took all the negative things I came across and turned them into my motivation to keep going and keep working. That's intrinsic motivation in action. That's what you want to instill in your employees. Create a motivation inside them to where they take pride and want to keep going and want to make the company better.

RESPECT

Respect is another goal. Just like with intrinsic motivation, if all the previous skills are effective, then you have succeeded. They will respect you. If you can successfully motivate people to do better at their jobs, then you will have their respect.

Gaining someone's utmost respect is a hard thing to accomplish. When there isn't respect for a leader, it is difficult to achieve follow-through with tasks. Respect is when a person acknowledges, admires, and values your thoughts and agendas. They support your opinions because they know you and your priorities. Your employees trust your decision making.

Only so much respect can be given due to someone's position or role within a company. Most times, respect must be earned. You can earn it by going above and beyond the call of your basic job requirements and doing more than you're told.

Respect, motivation, and innovation are the three most important things to focus on here, but the only way you can accomplish all these is if the other attributes are also present. They are the way you are going to succeed as a leader and as a company. All of these tactics placed together will drive any small or large business to success.

This is how young new leaders need to think, no matter what line of business you're in. This kind of leadership is the kind that gets you promoted and the kind that makes you successful.

14
Fostering Creativity and Innovation

Creativity and innovation are two of the most important assets to a company and a person. What do these mean? Creativity allows you to come up with the ground-breaking ideas. Then you employ a little innovation to move the concept from idea to product (or service). When used correctly, you get revolutionary results.

Take a moment and think about what actually moves a company forward. You might say acquiring new businesses or expanding into new industries or departments. Yes, these do create more profit, but if you really want to move forward and control the market, then you need to change the approach. You need to think about creating a market. The best way to control the market is when you create one and set the bar for your competitors.

Apple did a fantastic job of this years ago when the company first released the iPod Touch.

Never before had a company released a product that was so cutting-edge. They combined games, useful lifestyle apps, music, movies, and communication into one sleek, small profile. This was revolutionary and changed the game for all electronics manufacturers. Then, shortly after, the iPhone hit the market. Thus, the smartphone was born. They successfully created a new market and a new "need." Their intricate planning for the timing of the release dates and updates for the new products was perfect. This was all credited to their research and development program.

What is the one mistake that most smaller companies—and sometimes larger ones—make when the economy starts hurting their pocket? Almost instantly, lots of companies cut funding to the research and development teams. When you do this, your business is moving laterally or even negatively. Then people start to wonder why the stock isn't going back up. Well, it's because the company is trying to survive. In reality, it hurts more than it helps.

Think about it this way. My business installs and designs solar and wind installations. If we only kept up with constructing the normal flat solar panels everyone knows of today, would we be in business twenty years from now? When you start a business, you don't want it to be dead in the water long after you're gone, do you? Granted, some may not care at that point. But twenty years from now, we may be using dome-shaped solar panels. News flash: they're already being used. If these can be implemented as efficiently as they seem to be working, I'm going to be out of a job in ten to twenty years. That's not good.

Personally, if I'm going to place my name on something, it's going to receive all of the attention it needs. Just like my grandfather taught me about construction, I apply it to business. I hope that you can take this advice too, because it is all about holding yourself to a higher standard.

Imagine this scenario. It's now twenty years in the future. My client base has greatly depreciated because I was unable to keep up with the product growth.

I understand that this can be a tough decision for small operations. This is your call as a leader, but consider the possible consequences. There are billions of people in the world and everyone has ideas, but few have the ability or knowledge of how to act on it.

Funding is important, but it's not the only way to support creative and innovative ideas. A company should listen to the ideas of its employees. In my experience it can be worth it, because my ideas aren't always the best. For my business, one of my guys had a better idea for constructing a wind turbine. My way would have cost more money; his was significantly more efficient. Everyone needs to be open to one another for help.

A great example that I can personally speak for is Disney. They provide resources for their cast members so their ideas are heard. I have seen multiple times when frontline cast members wanted to implement a change. They followed the correct paths and after getting the approval, their ideas were used. Disney does a fantastic job of listening to their cast members, because they understand that they are the ones who are directly doing the work. If certain people see a positive change, they are always willing to hear more ideas.

I actually wanted to find out for myself how much creativity other large companies allowed their employees. So I interviewed managers and leaders from six national and international retail companies around the world. In every industry, from shoe brands and designer clothing companies to low-end retail clothing department chains, I found through personal interviews with employees of various levels that they have no freedom whatsoever. They can suggest ideas, but feedback (other than "You aren't allowed to do that") is rarely given. These companies all had some form of a visual team that was responsible for how everything looked.

For example, an employee noticed something was selling more. He wasn't allowed to place it on another shelf so the product could get more attention in the hopes of it selling even more. Another comment that was made referred to the layout of every store. The employee said that in winter the company made them place winter items at the front of the stores, but in Florida these kinds of jackets were not needed. This particular location wasn't selling many jackets due to the weather. Due to the company's strict policy on store layout, they were now losing premium space and possible profits. The company as a whole needs to be open to this kind of feedback instead of being so focused on the corporate structure. You can have structure and still value an employee's idea; you all work for the same company.

In my opinion, the businesses I interviewed should have handed over the creation of store displays to their employees. This would have solved the problems and created a large amount of new revenue, considering it was an international clothing chain. I understand that a company should have control over the visual perception of the store, but in my mind they should allow change, especially if the change brings along increased revenue.

INHIBITING CREATIVITY & INNOVATION

So this brings me to more things that inhibit creative flow and the innovative process. These are the things you want to avoid. If these things exist, make it your goal to eliminate them. Especially within leadership, it needs to be a top priority to focus on the work environment of your employees.

One of the biggest negative impacts to a work environment is office politics. Yes, we have all heard of it. Hopefully, we all hate it enough to put an end to it. Unfortunately, we know lots of people who don't. As leaders (and also as regular employees), we have decisions to make.

Try to remain as professional as possible. It is best to simply not get involved in the first place. There are those certain people who love to start everything; don't give them their way. Simply let them know that you're not getting involved in the situation.

I've been in situations where I have decided to not offer opinions to coworkers, because the work environment was so dramatic that I wanted absolutely no part of it. It's so hard to keep your thoughts to yourself. This is also a crucial part of being innovative. If you don't feel comfortable in your environment, you will be suppressed. Creative flow cannot be present in an environment where someone is worried about what other employees are saying about him or her. This is a manager's job to fix. Let the manager know if this is occurring.

All in all, just refrain from office gossip. You're too good for it, and you definitely won't get promoted for doing it. So figure out a better way to spend your time.

To build on coworkers' perceptions, don't worry about what they think about your ideas. Evaluations can get to employees' and leaders' heads sometimes. Your boss is not judging you on your ideas. It never hurts to give leadership your ideas or opinions. Hopefully they have created an environment that encourages employees.

Don't feel threatened by being compared to others' ideas. Don't compare yours to others. Why worry yourself? The simpler the idea, the more likely management will employ it. They tend to really like ideas that are easy to follow through with and require the least amount of funding. So there's no need to compare and frustrate yourself. Management will likely not compare you to your coworkers, either.

This is a common problem in the workplace. You should not fear getting negative criticism on your ideas. Critiques are what you want, because they let you know what you need to fix. Don't take it personally. Just keep thinking.

Another blockade to innovation in the workplace can be bad scheduling. We all have been there when we were understaffed. What was the focus during the whole shift? To get three jobs done at once, right? It probably seemed like you never got a break. In this case you never even had the chance to think about innovating your work environment. You were so busy and fixated on getting your tasks fulfilled that you didn't have the time.

From a leadership perspective, make sure that you use your resources wisely. Times such as these, when there are mismanaged resources, cause a distraction. If the right amount of employees and resources were allotted, then it causes a lot less stress at the job site. No one is worried, and there is a sense of comfortableness. When your employees are comfortable, that's when the ideas flow.

So now you seem to have eliminated most of the relational environmental issues. These make up most of the workplace distractions that take away from innovative thinking. These next few have to do with communication within leadership and the hierarchy.

The first has to do with consistency. Keep the goals of your workplace the same. Don't be constantly changing your plans or goals. It's OK to periodically change the emphasis on your products or services, but stick with a select few for a period of time. Change is a great thing, but don't change too often. You don't want your employees to give up on innovative thinking due to a constantly changing environment.

This last one is related to the study I did, which I described at the beginning of the chapter. Avoid controlling upper management. You don't want to give the impression that employees have limited freedom to share their creativity. Open the playing field to them. Let them know that their ideas are welcomed. That is the point of what you're trying to accomplish.

Some individuals also feel that they have no control over their idea once they have relinquished it. This is one of those situations you can't really help. In some instances they may ask for your opinion, but in the big picture, upper management is in control. This is one thing you kind of have to deal with when you tell your ideas to the company.

These are the areas that are most known to decrease innovation. Assess your own workplace and see what can be fixed. Management is there to help. Maybe even encourage them to support creative ideas from the employees. This is the only way business will grow.

SUPPORTING CREATIVITY & INNOVATION

Now here's what to do right. You need to strive and create a work environment free of negative distractions, essentially eliminating the problems mentioned in the previous section. Now that the environment is a productive one, you can begin to enact change. The change begins with the leadership within the company. In order for your employees to believe in it, you have to believe in it.

The fastest way to instill innovation and creativity within a company is for upper management to make it a priority. This type of flow is key for a company's success. This decision is a corporate one, and it flows from the top down. It is extremely hard to try and influence a new change or emphasis if it starts from the bottom. I'm not saying it can't be done, but if you're in a position at the top, take it. Find a way to drive employees to want to do better and make their company more successful. But remember: effective change starts from the top.

Innovation must be a priority. The company's future planning and orientation also needs to be a constant focus. These priorities are all one and the same. Innovation is the future of your company, but at the same time, conceptual planning of the company's future orientation sparks innovation. This is usually used as more of a cause rather than an effect of innovative business practice.

The best way to promote innovation and conceptual thinking without directly doing so is through challenges. Give your employees something challenging to work on. Tasks like this that require deep thought will produce deep work. This gets the mind thinking about things that otherwise it may not. If employees are crunched for time while working on a challenging project, it also helps them to be more efficient. They tend to focus more on how the simplest way of accomplishing the task is done.

Now, remember the problem mentioned at the beginning having to do with the visual display teams? Employees need to have a voice, and that voice can't be heard if it is being suppressed. You don't want employees to be scared from sharing their opinions. Open communication is a great thing to have in an office—a community where lower-level employees can communicate with higher-level leaders. Now, there are some instances where this may not be able to occur, but the key word here is communication. Simply keeping up-to-date with your employees in a friendly, approachable manner is important. This instills that feeling of comfort so that they can feel free to share their ideas.

Another way to help create an encouraging environment is by showing pride in your employees. If you take pride in their actions and celebrate the good things they do, they will have a higher output in their job position. A great way to help them reach their potential is by recognizing their efforts. Recognition encourages a certain behavior. When you recognize your employees for doing something great, they want to continue to do it. This is easy and cost-effective. A nonmonetary reward is great. It recognizes them for a specific task. In the end, a reward is a reward and they'll feel good about their work no matter what. This drives their potential, which gives them a sense of pride in what they do. Hopefully this motivates your employees to perform better.

If you put these strategies to work, what do you get? What is the result among your peers? What is the result within your company? Your area or department will have an increased flow of productivity—productivity that was encouraged through recognition, pride, challenges, potential, and low amounts of drama. You have now succeeded. But what have you inadvertently created? You've just instilled intrinsic motivation within your workforce. This is motivation that can be created only from within someone. This is what allows a person to be motivated from the inside. It is the part of you that sets goals and doesn't stop until they are accomplished. You have successfully created an environment where creativity and innovation can freely flow.

Once the environment is there, it's time to get the ball rolling. Learning is that little thing as kids that we didn't want to do after we left high school. Well, here it is again. When we stop learning, we stop innovating. Individually and institutionally we need to drive creativity, innovation, and learning. Learning not only from our mistakes and shortcomings but from our consumers.

15
Investing in Your Asset: You

You are the most valuable asset you have, specifically your mind and your heart.

When ideas come to mind, who drives them?
When employees need help, who guides them?
You want to be the solution to all problems and inquiries. There are many different ways to help yourself when it comes to bettering your odds. Not all leaders are created equal. There are passive ones, optimistic ones, aggressive ones, strategic ones, and conceptual ones. There is no specific leadership style that is perfect, because every industry needs to be driven differently.

This section is here to leave you with things that you can do to help yourself. These are lots of personal lessons I have learned growing up and through various business ventures. There are also going to be some ways that you can help yourself to develop certain habits that ambitious people possess.

The sooner you begin to help yourself, the sooner you can begin a life of doing what you love. Earlier in the book I began with a statement. I want you to remember it when it becomes hard for you to keep persevering.

Your goal is to create a life that you never have to take a vacation from.

When times get to be a struggle, this helps me a lot. You don't want a life where you look for the weekend or a vacation. You want something that you can enjoy for what it's worth. View it as a journey. Here is how I would go about it.

QUALITIES TO PURSUE

These are ways to better yourself as a person and develop yourself as a leader. Utilize them well, and they are sure to help you become who you want to be one day. I have created a list of nine essential ways to set yourself up as a dedicated and motivated leader. They are:
Networking
Being Proactive
Being Responsible
Being Informative-Knowledgeable
Being Dedicated
Being Competitive
Being Innovative

Communicating Well/Being Courteous
Winning Others Over
Being Driven

The strengths I have listed above are all ways you can help yourself grow. If you're like me, you don't like to waste time. My parents taught me some of these when I was growing up, and they have come to be a great blessing. I would like to share them with you.

NETWORKING

Connecting with people is what business leaders do. Businesses can get in tough situations sometimes, and you may have to rely on your connections. In the business world, the more you can integrate other resources to get the job done, the more effective and productive you will be.

Yes, I've mentioned that word again in this short book. You may be wondering why I'm mentioning this subject again after I wrote a chapter about the importance of it. It's because it's just that important. Knowing someone can be the difference between getting a job and not. If you want to one day move up in a company, you need to put yourself in front of those people you want to become. They are the ones who will be the key to you moving up.

At some point in your life you have probably met someone where you said, "Wow, I want to have your job one day. How did you get there?" That's exactly what you should be doing. Create a dialogue with these kinds of people. Don't let the conversation end there. Send them a thank-you note after you meet them. It may be meaningful to them, because no one takes the time to handwrite a letter anymore. I know I would be flattered to get one.

The key here is to stay in contact with those interesting people you meet on a daily basis. You never know — you just might end up working for them one day.

BEING PROACTIVE

There are proactive people, and there are reactive people. Reactive people wait till something happens to go into action. Proactive people get the motions going in the right direction. Being reactive can be a good thing, but being proactive is more important. If a leader is proactive, he or she tries to anticipate the needs of employees and clients. Having proactive leadership can potentially prevent negative situations in the workplace.

BEING RESPONSIBLE

Showing responsibility is a very important thing. Responsibility comes with trust. When people see that you are responsible and know how to accomplish a task, they in return can trust you. As you develop into a professional person, being responsible and trustworthy are two great qualities to practice.

Think of a retail store, for example. They depend on honest cashiers in order to keep their revenue flowing. They rely on them to not steal. If they couldn't have the slightest amount of trust in their responsible employees, then they couldn't even function as a business.

As you start out in an entry-level job, show your leaders or managers how you can get the job done. Offer to help in any way possible.

As I grew up, I always asked managers if they needed an extra hand to get tasks done. Whatever the answer was, I always said that I'd do it. Even if I didn't know how to do it, I said yes. If I didn't know how to get the job done, then I asked someone who did and learned how to do it. I quickly made a reputation for myself as being a doer. Everywhere I have ever worked I did this. I showed my employers and my employees that I could be trusted to get the job done, no matter what it was.

I highly encourage doing this. It has worked great for me. I can tell you it impresses me when an employee faces a task head-on that he or she has never done before. It shows confidence. From a leadership perspective, it's very impressive. Do this as often as possible.

BEING INFORMATIVE-KNOWLEDGEABLE

Knowing everything about what you're doing is extremely important—not just for the knowledge itself, but to be useful. Staying up-to-date is the main point.

When you're dealing with customers, they're going to want useful information. It only helps you to be able to do this. It can't hurt. Your coworkers will also appreciate this. Everyone brings something different to the table. This is an easy way to be a resource in your workplace.

This can help not only at work, but in getting a job as well. Research the company, its major accomplishments, recent changes in the industry, and find ways where you can contribute. Showing your knowledge of the market and industry will set you apart from the other potential hires.

Industry knowledge will also help you with your own projects. Investors and clients will feel more comfortable.

Get into this. It shows everyone that you care about what you do. It shows dedication. Employers like to see employees that take pride in their company and want to learn more about what it does.

BEING DEDICATED

Have you ever heard of believing in your brand? Well, if you haven't, I would say it's time you did. Believing in your brand is basically saying that you're dedicated to your company. In other words, you know why you all stand out among the rest.

Employees who believe in their brand exemplify dedication. They are the ones who can sell their product or service to anybody. They are also the ones that on a regular basis go above and beyond in the workplace. They do more than they're asked.

Dedication is a commitment to your job and the name or brand that you work for. I'm not saying you can only use a certain brand of dish soap in your house if you work for that certain brand. But it helps, because you can honestly represent your company.

When you have dedication, you can be a more effective employee, spouse, father, etc. It's not just in business.

As you enter the workforce, find ways to be able to dedicate yourself to your job, at least during work hours. Find ways to go the extra mile. Then watch how much it gets noticed. I promise if you keep this up, any diligent manager will recognize it. Just maybe they'll save that promotion with your name on it.

BEING COMPETITIVE

Competition is healthy. I'm not saying that creating teams in the workplace is something you need to implement. Competition is about setting small goals and pushing yourself to be proactive in achieving them. You will learn a lot about your drive and perseverance through this.

Practice setting small and large goals. Make it an objective to get the job done. See how hard it is for you to accomplish them. Through small exercises like this, you will learn a lot from yourself.

Try to set goals to complete your tasks in a timely manner. Use your time wisely and seek ways of making things easier and better for your coworkers. However, don't sacrifice your job quality when initializing this skill set.

BEING INNOVATIVE

Innovation is a major quality that I believe everyone should practice. I have worked in many different work environments from retail, pipeline construction, alternative energy, and oil companies. Try to be innovative wherever you go. I always try to think of ways to make a certain system or procedure better. If I find a way, I speak out. Again, this shows that you care enough about your job to try and help the company. Doing things like this never hurts you.

Try thinking on a daily basis of how to improve certain tasks. We see infomercials on TV almost every day about a new vacuum or blender. The people who created these products were doing this exact thing. They are innovators that were simply trying to improve a process. They implemented their idea, and now they are selling it to you.

COMMUNICATING WELL/ BEING COURTEOUS

This is huge. Communication is the way humans interact with one another. Communication is the way you express relationships between people. A good manager has built steady relationships with his or her employees. A good manager takes an interest in his or her employees.

You may not be a manager yet, but you can start practicing now. Get to know your coworkers on a personal level. Try to find what their wants are. Show that you care.

One of the most important things you can also do is be courteous. It's easy for managers to get into a routine where things can go unrecognized. Build a habit while you're young of showing your gratitude and appreciation toward everyone. I have heard it said before in relation to a question. The question was, "What is the name of the janitor?" Janitorial work tends to be thought of as a small job, but it isn't. The point of this question is to make you think about stepping out of your department and showing appreciation to people who otherwise may not receive any. If you thank people for simply smiling at a customer or cleaning a window, watch how fast they become happier with their job. Watch how much pride they take in their job.

WINNING OTHERS OVER

Before I get a chance to explain, don't take this the wrong way. Winning others over (WOO) is a skill that very few are able to master. Have you ever heard of wooing a woman? (WOOing — get it?) Well, it kind of plays on the same concept.

This has to do with the ability to gain support for your cause. It has to do a lot with persuasion. It means that you are good at getting people on your side. You gain support easily.

This is something that you can practice. Don't let people just see the person you are at work. For lack of a better explanation, allow them to see that you have a brain, and that you're more than just a methodical employee.

When people know what you're capable of, they think highly of you. Let them see more than simply what they are required to see.

Be the answer to problems and show them that you deserve more than where you're at. No one else knows your possibilities unless you show them.

BEING DRIVEN

Having drive is very closely related to being dedicated. They feed off each other. You're probably getting tired of hearing me mention drive and motivation for the millionth time.

I am repeating this because it is the most important thing you can take from this book. Along with networking, your motivation is the only thing that you can employ within yourself to make a difference.

All the qualities and skill sets I have mentioned so far are learnable. You can learn any of these. Being able to instill intrinsic motivation within yourself and others is more of a born skill. This isn't to say that it can't be learned. It can be hard, though. This is why I suggest that you start as soon as possible.

Encouragement, faith, and trust in others are good ways to instill motivation in others. When they see that someone supports them in what they are doing, it helps them want to continue doing a good job. Find ways to say "thank you" and "good job." These little words can go a long way.

All of these characteristics can be taught and learned. From experience it is harder for leaders to effectively learn them if they haven't much experience utilizing them. It can be done, but it takes some dedication. The earlier you practice these, the better.

There is one trait that makes what some people call a natural-born leader. The quality that makes natural leaders different is their character. Character can be taught, but like other things, takes dedication.

If you can learn how to motivate yourself, you can do anything. Motivation and drive get the job done. Motivation can be learned, so practice early. It also helps to assign a personal value to your work, because then you have a drive to do well. I always think about if I had to place my name on it, how do I want my work to appear? Have pride in what you do.

16
What to Look for in a Company

Not many people are going to pursue their ideas before they even have a job. This section is here to help you better search for the company you want to be a part of. I will share with you the five things I look for when evaluating companies and how well I would fit into their work environment.

I prefer companies that have primary focuses on innovation and development. If you're like me, you'll make that a priority. I want to be a part of something that is going to change the world. I view companies' performance in five different criteria:

Hiring and Recruiting
Leadership Decision Making
Recognition
Internal Communication
Failure Rate

These factors can help you analyze a company to see how innovative it actually is. These are also five factors you can use to evaluate your own company. If you start something new and want to keep developing, keep this in mind as you expand as well. These five important areas are what will create the persona of your company.

HIRING AND RECRUITING

When on the job hunt, what do you look for? The first people you come in contact with are the job recruiters or the people responsible for interviewing and hiring. Have you ever thought about how this looks to those outside the company, rather than internally?

It's easy from a managerial standpoint to sit back and decide what characteristics and qualities you want in an employee. Now, try to analyze it from the potential new employee's perspective.

When you interview at a certain company, what kinds of things are the recruiters looking for in you? You don't want to go with the first company and undercut your value. The first step is to know your self-worth. You want them to value your specific expertise and not just view you as a set of shoes to fill. You want to look for a company that has an agenda and that can employ your qualities to work for them.

You want to work for a company that uses the talent they have available—a company that will work with you on your aspirations to grow within the company.

LEADERSHIP DECISION MAKING

How does company leadership function? Do they communicate effectively? Do they assign tasks just to get the job done, or do they take the time to consider the right employee for the job? How does communication function between upper management and lower-level employees?

These are all important areas that can make or break your work experience. Try to examine how tasks are assigned. See if employees' skill sets fit the roles they are performing.

It can be hard to observe this function without being a part of the company. If possible, it is worth asking about, though, to make sure that the company is a good fit for you.

RECOGNITION

This should be an important focus for a business. I mentioned my views on this earlier. From a management standpoint, this is a very powerful tool to utilize in order to help promote employee morale and production.

From your point of view as a new hire, you want to look at how the company recognizes different achievements. There will be times during your career when you will question why you're still there. Sometimes your benefits and the recognition of achievements and anniversaries can be key motivators for you.

Recognition gives you an intrinsic value. When inquiring about a company's recognition program, try to evaluate how a company views and respects certain achievements. Keep in mind, too, if you ever want to transfer to another company or division, recognitions and awards can show the hiring committee what you've accomplished. Recognition is not just for motivating yourself and others, but to also give yourself a boost when it comes to applying for a promotion or new position.

INTERNAL COMMUNICATION

This is the first quality I look for in a company. If this is going to be my work environment, how do I want it to be? Keep in mind that communication that encourages innovation is always open.

You want leadership to be a walk down the hall or an e-mail away. If you're like me, you want to be able to communicate with other lines of business. You want to be able to meet your boss's boss. Executives aren't some mythical creatures, so don't treat them as something you can never become. Start a career at a place where you can have relationships with upper management.

Your career is about who you know.

Communication between employees and management needs to be consistent. It needs to be welcoming. New ideas need to be encouraged. Most importantly, employees need to have access to the people who can implement their ideas. Otherwise, innovation will not be present.

FAILURE RATE

We hear often how companies claim to have low failure rates, but are they really grasping the point? Companies that claim to have a high success rate are failing themselves. I would stay away and be wary of companies like these. It seems like they have something to hide.

So, you're probably wondering why I'm making this outrageous claim, right? Well, it's because true innovation doesn't always have success. In fact, you're going to fail more than you win, but when you win, you win big. There's a quote that I love by Dean Kaanan, the inventor of the Segway. He said, "Less failure equals less innovation." I agree with him 100 percent.

To me, claims of having high success rates means that a company is fearful. They don't take enough risks on revolutionary products that will create a new industry. They settle for more realistic ideas that don't take much effort and consider that a success. Don't get me wrong; that is short-term success, but in the long run, they're only cheating themselves.

You want to choose a company that not only claims to support innovative ideas, but also follows through. You can tell which companies these are. They're the ones that have emerged at the top of their industries and have continued to remain dominant for the past twenty to forty years. These are the innovative ones. No one has outperformed them yet, and it is because they took appropriate risks.

Very few people have worked for themselves and no one else. Most of the time, you'll find yourself working two or three jobs to try to earn enough money to fund your dreams and aspirations. It isn't always cost-effective to be an innovator, entrepreneur, or inventor. People look at us as smart and gifted people. We are intelligent, but we're driven people as well. We know and understand how to motivate ourselves and do whatever it takes to make it happen.

17
It's Time...

I mentioned in the very beginning of my book that I'm a futurist. I hope by now it is obvious to how I perceive the world as opportunity waiting for us to make a change. Everyone has a different paradigm. I see things different from you. Possible business partners and investors will see things different from you. Most people aren't going to be used to seeing things as uniquely as you do. Often times they will tend to criticize your ambition. They are the ones who need to stop their ignorance from accepting change. So, go ahead show the world what you bring to the table.

It's time for you to begin your own journey. Congratulations, because you've already started by being intrigued enough to simply finish this novel. Now you have a taste for what is ahead. Go grab it for yourself, and feed your hunger.

This book serves as a good example of starting on your journey. I wrote it with the goal of helping other young adults achieve their full potential. Before now, I never considered myself to be a writer or even a reader for that matter. I honestly never enjoyed reading if I wasn't reading to gain information or to learn a new subject. As I became more dedicated and motivated towards the goal of publishing, I did everything necessary to get this book in your hands. Through all of the cold mornings spent from 4-7 AM sitting on my balcony bundled up in clothes with my coffee and laptop in hand. It wasn't easy and it took commitment to make this happen, and right now I can tell you it was well worth it.

I've taken you through my story, told you how I went about it, and taught you some ways you can help yourself. Apply these things. Keep in mind there is no set path to find success in the things you love.

Each of us are on our own unique adventure. We both possess our own strengths. Focus on what you do best and change the way it is done. Create a new industry if you have to. That's a real revolutionary idea there.

As you embark, stay focused on your goals. My parents and teachers used to always say, "Keep your eyes on the prize." Don't lose sight of where you want to be, because a temporary cloud of doubt disrupts your view. It's easy to become complacent with where you are in life, especially as a young adult. At this point you tend to have lots of debt coming out of college, and also the shock of life on your own. This can make your dreams and visions foggy. Have some faith. Keep your head up. See where you're wanting to go, and get there. Be a difference maker.

You have a plan created for your life. It's your job to discover it. I'm just beginning mine and firmly believe that the best is yet to come. I have to remain actively looking for opportunities to make a difference. Confidence and determination are going to be the fuel. When times get tough and adversity strikes, it becomes hard to see where you're going. This is the hindrance for most people. There will be lots of nay-sayers or haters out there. As soon as someone sees you have your eyes on something better than them, they will begin to tear you down. News flash, people like you and me aren't going to change our path for their lack of vision and motivation. It doesn't affect our plans, it just makes it sweeter.

Like I mentioned earlier; there are evolutions, innovations, and revolutions. Whatever it takes, reach for it as if you would for your last breath. You'll find success when you want it as bad as you need to breathe. You're the only one that can guide your life. Make the most of it.

Now you have read the beginning of my story, I hope to hear yours.

Printed in Great Britain
by Amazon